The Military and Society

REVIEWS OF RECENT RESEARCH

The Military and Society

REVIEWS OF RECENT RESEARCH

**Trends in History
Volume 2, Number 2**

Copublished by
The Institute for Research in History and The Haworth Press

The Haworth Press, Inc., 28 East 22 Street, New York, New York 10010.

Library of Congress Cataloging in Publication Data
Main entry under title:

The Military and society.

(Trends in history, ISSN 0270-790X ; v. 2, no. 2)
Includes indexes.
1. Sociology, Military—Addresses, essays, lectures. I. Series.

U21.5.M447	306'.2	81-20073
ISBN 0-917724-44-5		AACR2

CATJun18'83

6-03-83 ABS 23.95 Boettcher

82-6791

The Military and Society

Trends in History
Volume 2, Number 2

Contents:

PREFACE

The relationship between the military and society is evident to anyone who picks up the morning newspaper and reads the most recent story on the B-1, the Trident, or the MX. Each of these weapons systems is a topic of intense debate affecting the national budget, environment, and economy. Similar debates occur in other countries, although not always in public, and have occurred in the past, even in antiquity. No one who reads *The Peloponnesian War* by Thucydides, that brilliant analysis of Greek society at its apogee, can overlook the nexus between soldier and civilian, military and society.

Given the general agreement on the interdependence and mutual influence of the two spheres, it would be reasonable to assume that there should be a thriving historical field for its study. And, indeed, the bibliography of books and articles on the military itself and on aspects of its relationship to society is huge. There is, however, no clearly identified field called military and society, nor any field that examines that area under another name. Military historians, narrowly defined, rarely try to relate their material to broader social issues. Social historians tend to concentrate on society and leave the military to the military historians. Military figures who enter politics are mainly the domain of political historians and, more recently, psychohistorians; and so forth. What could be one of the most important fields of history is, in fact, not a field at all, because its components have been appropriated and carried off by specialists of one sort or another.

And yet the materials abound for major synthetic works on the military and society treated as a unified field, as will become evident to the reader of this volume of *Trends in History*. Tanenbaum's essay on France is a study in the political interactions of government and army. Menze's article shows how the military has become part of the great debate on continuity vs. discontinuity in the history of modern Germany. Brown and Lovett emphasize the importance of the Italian armed forces as instruments of national, social, and linguistic unity, functions which have justified the existence of the military establishment even when it could not successfully wage war. Pintner's Russia before the Revolution contains armies in which peasants labored at many of the same tasks they would have pursued had they been allowed to stay on their farms; the relationship of civilian life to military

1

was painfully obvious to contemporary critics. Peasants in Mao's Red Army, however, were if anything a source of strength, both to the military narrowly defined and to the Communist movement in general, as Strand and Chan make clear. Greene's study of women during World War II pulls together the extant scholarship to provide historical insights and raise provocative questions. The close interaction of war with American politics and foreign policy is evident from the essay by English. Coffman, treating U.S. history from the social and military perspective, notes that "armies and navies do not cease to exist between wars and . . . have effects that are not limited to the battlefield."

The raw material exists, therefore, for an historical discipline called military and society, and these *Trends* essays suggest some ways to proceed. One beginning has already been made by the Military and Society Seminar of The Institute for Research in History, which began meeting in November of 1981. Other seminars and workshops will doubtless be established by groups around the country, for few fields are so timely and so likely to yield significant results.

William Zeisel
The Institute for Research
in History

THE FRENCH ARMY AND THE THIRD REPUBLIC

Jan Karl Tanenbaum

In separate articles, historians André Martel and André Corvisier ("Le renouveau de l'histoire militaire en France" [*Revue historique*, DXVII, 1971, 107-126] and "Aspects divers de l'histoire militaire" [*Revue d'histoire moderne et contemporaine*, XX, 1973, 1-9]) note that French military scholars have traditionally examined French military history from a single perspective: battles, fortifications, and campaigns—the "drum and trumpets" type of history. There have been few articles, monographs, and books that relate the French army to wider social, political, and economic considerations.

The basic reason for this shortcoming is that disciplines such as sociology, psychology, economics, and political science were seldom taught in the pre-World War II universities. The French historians who were trained in the 1930s and who dominated their field in the post-World War II period tended to follow traditional methods of research and presentation. Second, the experience of World War I assured that there would be widespread interest in the minute description of the countless battles, whether small or large. It should be noted that American historians have recognized the shortcomings of this narrow approach. Concentrating on the relationship of the army to political and social concerns, Americans have made a major contribution to 20th-century French military history.

Martel and Corvisier agree that a gradual change has been taking place within the field. French military historians are placing military events within the context of the contemporary political and social setting. The single greatest reason for the change was France's catastrophic 1940 defeat. In an attempt to explain this defeat, historians began to focus upon nonmilitary factors such as an inadequate educational system, economic retardation, and a politically and economically divided society. The second reason for the change was the French army's frequent intervention into the political realm in the late 1950s and early 1960s.

Both Martel and Corvisier observe that most of the recent French publications in this "new" military history have dealt with the *Ancien Régime*. And for good reason. The 50-year archival rule has until recently tended to discourage research in the army of the Third Republic (1870-1940). Now, however, as the restrictions are being lifted, French doctoral students are beginning to examine the army of the Third Republic. Unfortunately, the very nature of the French doctoral program, which requires a decade or more of research, means that much of the fruit of this work has not yet been published. If the preliminary dissertation lists are any indication of the studies currently being done, the wait will be well worth while. The impact will be twofold: French traditional military historians will not recognize the field; and American historians will be overwhelmed if only because, for obvious reasons, they will have difficulty competing with French scholars at the archival level.

This essay will focus upon two aspects of the Third French Republic's army: the relationship between the state and the army, and French strategy at the outbreak of World War I and World War II.

In September 1870 at Sedan the Prussian army destroyed the army of Louis Napoleon's Second Empire. A few days later Paris proclaimed the creation of the Third Republic. In a pioneering work, *La société militaire dans la France contemporaine, 1815-1939* (Paris, 1953), Raoul Girardet points out that despite the shattering defeat of 1870, the French officer corps maintained its position for the next 30 years as a nearly autonomous body, unfettered by direct civilian control. Although republicans and monarchists could not agree on a wide range of religious and political issues during the early years of the Third Republic, they did have one area of fervent agreement—the reorganization and strengthening of the French army.

Monarchists, whether landed Bourbons or middle-class Orleanists, did not consider the army and the officer corps responsible for the defeat at Sedan. Instead, the conservatives hailed the army as the courageous victor over Paris and the 1871 Commune. The army, as it had demonstrated during the 1848 June Days, was once again the savior of the established social and economic order. The republicans also rallied around the army. The army was to be the vehicle by which France would once again be a great power; a strong army was a prerequisite if France were to recapture Alsace and Lorraine.

Girardet emphasizes that during the first decades of the Third Republic, the French officer corps' political attitudes were characterized by an antipathy to parliamentary institutions. The officer corps considered republican and military ideals irreconcilable; the military ethic of obedience and respect was thought to be undermined by the republican ideal of liberty and equality. These conservative attitudes were reinforced by the influx of aristocracy entering Saint-Cyr, the elite military college, during the first decades of the Third Republic. The economic depression of the 1870s and the 1880s forced many of the sons of the traditional nobility to seek a career other than on the land. Furthermore, as the administrative and political positions of the state were arrogated by the republicans, the army—the only public institution not republicanized—remained a source of employment and power for the aristocracy.

Despite these antirepublican sentiments, Girardet forcefully argues that the army was a politically neutral, disciplined bureaucracy. The officer corps did not support General Georges Boulanger in the late 1880s when the nationalists and monarchists urged the popular Boulanger to overthrow the Third Republic. And a decade later, the source of the civilian-army clash during the Dreyfus Affair, when a military court convicted an innocent Jewish officer of treason, was not the result of the army's attempts to intervene in the political arena. Precisely the opposite. The High Command refused to reconsider Dreyfus' outrageous conviction because the army resented civilian interference in what was considered to be a strictly military affair.

Although the army exercised no overt political role during the first decades of the Third Republic, Girardet fails to emphasize that the army exerted tremendous leverage upon the civilian government. The source of this power was threefold. First, the army refused to support the regime on a partisan basis. There is some doubt whether the army would have prevented Boulanger from overthrowing the Republic. Second, the army claimed priority and prestige because of its seniority. The army, which had existed long before the Republic, claimed that it represented the traditions of France and the nation more accurately than the recently created Republic. Third, the army had a functional importance that the Republic needed in a hostile world.

Girardet also fails to focus upon some disturbing aspects of the Dreyfus Affair: anti-Semitism, antidemocratic rumblings within the officer corps, and signs that discipline within the officer corps was beginning to crumble. These characteristics link France's army of 1900 with its army of 1940, the last days of the Third Repbulic.

A. S. Kanya-Forstner in *The Conquest of the Western Sudan: A Study in French Military Imperialism* (Cambridge, 1969) reminds us that nowhere was prewar civilian control of the army so totally lacking as in the colonies. In the 1880s and 1890s colonial commanders frequently disregarded orders from Paris and conquered vast territories at a time when the official colonial policy in Paris was based upon consolidation, not expansionism. As they drove into the interior of western Africa, justifying each additional conquest on the grounds of security, colonial officers often brutalized the native population, while the Colonial Office in Paris urged a policy of fostering commerce and trade with the native population. The colonial army's free and almost unlimited reign accentuated a disdain within the officer corps for civilian institutions; it also served to make the interior of western Africa an economically unproductive backwater within the French colonial empire.

David Ralston's *The Army of the Republic: The Place of the Military in the Political Evolution of France, 1871–1914* (Cambridge, Mass., 1967) has been greatly influenced by Girardet's view of the army as a nonpolitical, benign, and obedient servant of the state. Ralston, however, makes a useful contribution when he discusses the French army during the decade prior to World War I. Immediately following the Dreyfus Affair, republicans and socialists sought to republicanize the officer corps in an attempt to lessen the army's autonomy within the state. Some steps were successful, such as forcing the resignation of a couple of antirepublican generals and transferring the promotion process from the General Staff to the civilian War Ministry. But the attempt to change the political coloration of the officer corps failed: wholesale personnel purges, at a time of heightened international tensions with Germany, would have been unrealistic. Following the Second Moroccan Crisis of 1911, the army's prestige, independence, and popular support reached a level comparable to the position that it had held in the 1870s and 1880s. French politicians and the officer corps had the same major object: the rapid preparation for war.

Widespread popular support for the army did not mean that in August 1914, when World War I broke out, Frenchmen left feverishly for the front "with a flower in their guns." Jean-Jacques Becker, in one of the latest of the "new" military studies, *1914: Comment les français sont entrés dans la guerre* (Paris, 1977), analyzes in 600 pages French public opinion in August and September 1914 in order to determine to what degree Frenchmen supported the declaration of war. After examining the sentiments of church, political, professional, and labor groups, as well as towns and villages, he concludes that there was no nationalist fever to support the war. France was patriotic, not nationalistic. Frenchmen united around the idea of national defense in order to stop aggression.

Antimilitarism was nonexistent in 1914. Two regional studies, one by Roland Andréani ("L'Antimilitarisme en Languedoc méditerranéen avant la première guerre mondiale" [*Revue d'histoire moderne et contemporaine*, XX, 1973, 104-123]), and the other by J.-R. Maurin ("'Le Combattant lozérien de la classe 1907 lors de la première guerre mondiale" [*Revue d'histoire moderne et contemporaine*, XX, 1973, 124-135], emphasize that mobilization in 1914 went smoothly. Only about one per cent of the draftees failed to answer induction notices. There were no protests or demonstrations even in those regions where antimilitarism and anarchism had had a long history. Clearly, trade unionists, peasants, and the urban and provincial bourgeoisie joined in a common effort against a common enemy.

Future research on the French army will surely focus upon an analysis of the social and political composition of the officer corps. The recruitment and promotion procedures must also be examined. Such a study should illuminate some of the reasons for the frequent tensions between the army and the Third Republic. France was a democracy, yet the officer corps tended to be antidemocratic in outlook. Other than memoirs and contemporary observations, the only political and social analysis of the pre-World War I officer corps is François Bédarida's limited study for the 1870s, "L'Armée et la règublique: les opinions politiques des officiers français en 1876-78" (*Revue historique*, CCXXXII, 1964, 119-164). Bédarida uncovered records kept by local republican politicians and administrators, who apparently spied on the top echelons of the officer corps. Basing his study upon these dubious observations and opinions, Bédarida concludes that a large minority of the officer corps was drawn from the aristocracy while a sizeable majority was royalist and Bonapartist. Despite these sentiments, officers such as General Gallifet accepted the Republic because economically and socially it was very conservative; after all, it was republican France which had crushed the radical Paris Commune in 1871. Furthermore, the army and the Republic had the same goal: to regain Alsace and Lorraine.

A second area of growing research for the pre-World War I period deals with the failure of the French command to anticipate the Schlieffen Plan. Henry Contamine in *La Revanche, 1871-1914* (Paris, 1957) and Samuel R. Williamson, Jr. in *The Politics of Grand Strategy: Britain and France Prepare for War, 1904-1914* (Cambridge, Mass., 1969), in superb accounts of France's prewar military strategy, explain that when World War I broke out in August 1914, the French High Command had its forces facing east and northeast in anticipation that the main German attack would spring from Lorraine and Alsace. Instead, Germany poured 700,000 active and reserve troops into neutral Belgium. These German troops moved west of the Meuse and Sambre Rivers and then plunged south into France, out-flanking a stunned French army.

This wide envelopment maneuver through Belgium, while the rest of the German forces remained on the defensive in Alsace and Lorraine, is known as the Schlieffen Plan. It almost destroyed the French army in the first month of the war. Although the Battle of the Marne stopped the German offensive in September 1914, the initial success of the Schlieffen Plan was the major factor in determining that the Western Front of World War I would be fought in France's agricultural and industrial heartland. Germany's well-entrenched position deep in France resulted in the economic devastation of France, a high casualty rate for the French civilian population, and a high casualty rate for the French army because it unleashed several offenses in an attempt to drive the enemy out of the country. Had the Western Front been drawn along the Franco-German border, it is possible that an early peace agreement could have been reached. Fighting a war on German territory rather than 40 miles from Paris may have made the German High Command more receptive to a quick peace.

The question of course is why Generalissimo Joseph Joffre and the French High Command in 1914 failed to anticipate the Schlieffen Plan. Was it an intelligence breakdown? Or sheer stupidity on the part of the General Staff? Louis Garros in "Préludes aux invasions de la Belgique" (*Revue historique de l'armée,* V, 1949, 17-37) points out that as early as 1904 France was aware of the massive German rail building in the Aix-la-Chapelle area, right across from the Belgian border. France also received in 1904 the famous *Vengeur* documents, which detailed a German sweep through Belgium. In 1911 Generalissimo Victor Michel predicted a German move through Belgium. He correctly stated that Germany would have adequate manpower to fight from Switzerland to the Channel if it were to use its reserves in the front line. Michel wanted to do the same thing. He wanted to double the size of the French army by using the reserves in the front line and then to shift most of the French army to the Belgian border. But the French High Command rebelled against Michel and forced him to resign, while bringing Joffre to power as generalissimo. Joffre considered the reserves to be militarily worthless; therefore, he irrationally believed that the Germans would not use them in the front line. Without the reserves in the front line, the Germans would not have adequate manpower to pour massive troops into Belgium.

Why did the French High Command intensely dislike the reserves? Richard D. Challener offers a clue to the answer in *The French Theory of the Nation in Arms, 1866–1939* (New York, 1952). The question of reserves was interwoven with French prewar domestic politics. The Dreyfus Affair had convinced republicans and socialists that the officer corps threatened the existence of the Republic. Consequently, the French Left in 1905 reduced military service to two years. The Left sought to reduce the role of the active army as a body of troops already prepared to defend the nation. Instead, the army should be regarded as a training school in which the young conscripts learned the fundamentals of soldiering. It was assumed that the reservists would form the basis of the fighting army in case of war. On the other hand, the Right and the High Command feared that the 1905 Two Year Law was a major step toward the socialist ideal—the militia. In such a case the regular army would have been greatly diminished.

The vast literature on World War I focuses almost exclusively upon traditional military concerns such as campaigns and tactics. There are few exceptions. Jere Clemens King brilliantly sketches in *Generals and Politicians: Conflict between France's High Command, Parliament and Government, 1914–1918* (Berkeley, 1951) the wartime relationship between the High Command and the politicians. The great prestige which the army had enjoyed for centuries gave it an advantage over the civilian government at the outset of the war. Criticizing the High Command during the crucial weeks of August and September 1914, at a time when France was staving off the German invasion, would have been considered disloyal. The government and parliament deferred to Joffre and the army. Since a short war was anticipated, military supremacy over the civilian government would be of very short duration. As the war of attrition continued, however, and as the battles of Verdun, the Somme, and Chemin des Dames damaged the prestige of the High Command, the politicians gradually reasserted their control of the army. Having gone into the war under the quasi dictatorship of Joffre, France ended the war under the iron rule of Premier Georges Clemenceau, who was the champion of civilian primacy over the military.

Much of the wartime civilian-military drama centered upon General Maurice Sarrail. In *General Maurice Sarrail, 1856–1929: The French Army and Left-Wing Politics* (Chapel Hill, 1974), Jan Karl Tanenbaum explains how Sarrail, the only republican general with widespread left-wing support, was isolated within the upper echelons of the conservative officer corps. When Joffre removed Sarrail as commander of the Third Army in 1915, left-wing politicians rallied to Sarrail's support. If the wartime *union sacrée* were to survive, Sarrail must have a prominent command. Consequently, the government forced Joffre to appoint Sarrail commander of the Allied Eastern Army in the Balkans. Furthermore, it forced Joffre, who violently opposed removing French troops from the Western Front, to make a large-scale military commitment to the Balkans. Lastly, French left-wing politicians thwarted all of Joffre's attempts to remove Sarrail as commander of the Eastern Army. By constantly intervening in the military sphere, Sarrail's political supporters played a conspicuous role in reasserting political control over the High Command.

Military-civilian tensions, muted during the last year of the war, broke out afresh at the Paris Peace Conference. The conflict between Premier Clemenceau and Marshal Ferdinand Foch is described by Jere Clemens King in *Foch Versus Clemenceau: France and German Dismemberment, 1918–1919* (Cambridge, Mass., 1960). At the outset of the conference, Clemenceau and Foch both wanted to create an independent Rhineland state to serve as a buffer between France and Germany. Great Britain and the United States, speaking for the notion of self-determination, refused to permit the dismemberment of Germany. Clemenceau relented and accepted a compromise: a 15-year allied military occupation of the Rhineland and a security treaty with the United States and England. Clemenceau was willing to reject the idea of a buffer state because he realized that France's postwar security would be dependent upon the friendship and good will of the United States and England. Foch, however, refusing to accept Clemenceau's change of policy, threatened to resign if a Rhineland buffer state were not implemented. He rallied public opinion and prominent politicians in an attempt to force Clemenceau to reject President Wilson's compromise solution, and along with the French generals in the occupied Rhineland he attempted to create a Rhineland separatist movement in order to confront the "Big Three" with a fait accompli. Clemenceau's ability to overcome military opposition to his peace conference settlement was due to his recall to Paris of the recalcitrant generals in the Rhineland; his harsh reminder to Foch that the civilian government determined policy; and the failure of the separatist movement to win a large-scale following in the Rhineland, thereby destroying the popular French notion that the Rhinelanders wanted to separate from the rest of Germany.

The French *poilu* fought courageously during World War I. But in 1917, 30,000 to 40,000 French troops mutinied. Guy Pedroncini, in the most significant French work in recent decades dealing with World War I, *Les Mutineries de 1917* (Paris, 1967) minutely examines the 1917 military crisis. What were the causes of the mutinies? Revolutionary and pacifist propaganda, intensified by the March Russian revolution, did play a role. So did war weariness. But the basic cause was a lack of confidence in the High Command. The front-line soldier was totally disillusioned with the

High Command's method of warfare—repeated mass offensives with the hope of rupturing the German lines. Pedroncini convincingly maintains that the French soldier did not reject fighting, because even during the mutinies he repulsed all German attacks. The mutinies, instead, were a reaction to the hopeless attacks which had led to nothing but wholesale massacre. As a result of the mutinies, the French government rejected offensive warfare. French policy in the last year of the war was to remain on the defensive and wait for the Americans to arrive on the Western Front.

The experience of World War I shaped French military strategy during the interwar years and, according to Colonel Adolphe Goutard in *The Battle of France, 1940* (New York, 1959), it was largely responsible for the sudden French defeat in 1940. France's World War II strategy was based on defensive warfare; the Maginot Line—a string of bunkers along the eastern and northeastern border—was intended to keep the Germans at bay. The French High Command, again shaped by the experience of World War I, expected a long war of attrition. The economic strength of France and England, it was thought, would eventually prevail in a long war. The French High Command failed to appreciate the military potential of modern offensive warfare, especially the use of tanks and airplanes. In May 1940 Hitler would unleash these weapons to destroy the Third Republic.

Goutard's book is refreshing because the standard interpretations for the collapse of the Third Republic—economic, technological, sociological, and political factors—are minimized. The nonmilitary causes for the 1940 defeat were first put forth by the discredited French High Command. Goutard reminds us that the fall of France in 1940 was due to a military defeat. He maintains that despite its much maligned defensive strategy, France had an opportunity for victory. Unfortunately, the High Command was paralyzed by the memory of the horrors of World War I and plagued by its failure to understand what was happening on the battlefield. Specifically, Goutard insists that in September 1939, when the cream of the German army was on the Eastern Front, France should have invaded the Ruhr. Instead, France did nothing but wait. In May 1940 Hitler surprised France by attacking through the lightly guarded Ardennes; the French thought that the rolling terrain would prevent a large-scale tank invasion. The German Panzers broke through the French lines at Sedan (shades of 1870!) and then raced across northern France to the Channel in order to cut off the French army located in Belgium. Goutard points out that the German rush to the sea left a gap between the Panzer divisions and the major infantry units which were supposed to follow the tanks in order to cover

their flanks. The French had a golden opportunity to move into this cor-
ridor and to destroy the German armored divisions. Unfortunately, the
High Command failed to appreciate this tactical opportunity.

The French army's military incompetence helped to destroy the Third
Republic. This, however, should not obscure the fact that the French
officer corps played an important political role in the 1940 destruction of
democratic France; the French army in 1940 was involved in politics as
never before in the history of the Third Republic. Why did this occur?
Philip Bankwitz in *Maxime Weygand and Civil-Military Relations in
Modern France* (Cambridge, Mass., 1967) shows that during the interwar
period profound changes occurred in the traditional civilian-military relationship. The army shed its much heralded political neutrality and passive
obedience. The reasons for this transformation were many. In the 1930s a
large-scale nationalist Right, encouraged by the successes of Mussolini and
Hitler, emerged in France and looked to the army as the means to overthrow the Republic. February 6, 1934, when several hundred thousand
people protested against the Republic and forced the legally constituted
French government to resign, contained the germ of this new political
alliance between the veterans' organizations, part of the officer corps, and
antirepublican civilian groups. In addition, the French officer corps was
agitated by the specter of Communism, whether it was French attempts to
reach a military agreement with Soviet Russia or the existence of the
Popular Front government which depended upon French Communist support for its survival. Communism was synonymous with antimilitarism.
Finally, the moral authority of the Third Republic declined in the 1930s as
a result of mass political demonstrations, general strikes, political scan-
dals, and the government's failure to end the woes of the depression. The
army came forward as the guardian of the nation against the partisanship
and instability of the regime. The army would assure order and stability in
place of social revolution and disorder.

In May 1940, as the German army poured into France, the French
government appointed Maxime Weygand commander in chief of the
French army. Convinced that he was saving the state from ruin, Weygand
intervened directly in national politics. In early June he demanded that the
French government sign an armistice with Nazi Germany. Weygand, in an
act of disobedience, stated that he would refuse to fight if the French
government were to go to North Africa in order to continue the war against
Hitler. Without the support of its army, the French government had little
alternative but to seek an agreement with Nazi Germany. The Nazis immediately seized northern France, including Paris; the southern portion of

France—Vichy France—with General Weygand as war minister was a puppet state for Hitler.

Weygand's role in the 1940 catastrophe brought to a climax the tensions between the army and the Third Republic. Weygand's actions also foreshadowed the role of the French army during the next two decades. Charles de Gaulle in 1960 correctly noted the continuity between France's pre-World War I army and its army 50 years later: "The army—it was against Dreyfus; it was for Vichy; it was for Algerian integration [putschist and no independence for Algeria]."

Jan Karl Tanenbaum is on the faculty of Florida State University.

Journals Consulted

American Historical Review • English Historical Review • European Studies Review • French Historical Studies • History • Journal of Contemporary History • Journal of European Studies • Military Affairs • Revue de défense nationale • Revue d'histoire de la deuxième guerre mondiale • Revue d'histoire moderne et contemporaine • Revue historique • Revue historique de l'armée • Revue militaire générale.

THE MILITARY AND SOCIETY IN MODERN GERMANY: CONTINUITY AND CHANGE

Ernest A. Menze

Though the concepts of continuity and change have always been central to the historian's craft, there have been instances when the one or the other has become an "a priori straight jacket." Though much may be said for continuity in German history, the case for a coherent "continuity thesis" is still under question. Evidently the efforts of some historians to draw lines of continuity from Luther to Frederick the Great, Bismarck, and Hitler have raised more questions than they have answered in the examination of the 20th-century cataclysm.

Konrad H. Jarausch has persuasively defined the limits of the continuity thesis in German foreign policy ("From Second to Third Reich: The Problem of Continuity in German Foreign Policy" [*Central European History*, XII, 1979, 68–82]). He advises historians to avoid "the pitfalls of teleological reductionism," as well as the dangers of relativist apologia, by remembering that continuity must be viewed as the scholar's tool rather than as inherent to historical matter. Fritz Fischer's unequivocal indictment of German elites as the agents of continuity, recently reiterated in "Der Stellenwert des Ersten Weltkrieges in der Komtinuitätsproblematic der deutschen Geschichte" (*Historische Zeitschrift*, CCXXIX, 1979, 25–53) has been continuously subject to modifications such as those offered by Jarausch and the scholars cited by him. It is in this carefully restricted sense of continuity as a conceptual tool, balanced by the awareness of change, that the present article examines the recent periodical literature relative to the military and society in modern Germany.

Much of modern German history stands under the shadow of a military apparatus deemed essential to national survival. The absence of "natural frontiers" rendered Bismarck's *Reich,* not to speak of its Prussian nucleus, inexorably beholden to the armed forces as the guarantor of security. There is good cause, then, for the preeminent place consistently occupied by the military in the German value system. The continuity of this appreciation of the military, as well as the stresses caused by it, in a society not yet recovered from two disastrous total wars, was brought home to West Germany on the occasion of what has come to be known as the "Bremer Krawall," bloody riots accompanying the swearing in ceremony of 1,200 Bundeswehr recruits in the Bremen soccer stadium during the spring of 1980 (Nina Grunenberg, "Sozialdemokraten Sagen: 'Ohne uns': Der verpönte Zapfenstreich und die Debatte über Krieg und Frieden" [*Die Zeit,* XXXV, 23 May, 1980, 2]).

Although the disorders, which left 257 policemen injured, 23 of them seriously, were widely attributed to the conspiratorial activities of a minute ultra-leftist group, the *Chaoten,* the excesses of the riots and the public reaction to them helped focus the question of the relation between the military and society in the Federal Republic. While an increase in international tensions and inflammatory rhetoric concerning the aborted American rescue action in Iran all contributed to the riots, the events in Bremen and their discussion in the media revealed deeper cleavages in German society concerning its relationship with the military. For example, in "Young Rebels: A Psychopolitical Study of West German Male Radical Students" (*Comparative Politics,* XII, 1979, 27–48) S. Robert Lichter investigates the motivation of radical students such as those involved in the Bremer Krawall. His research among students at the universities of Tübingen and Konstanz confirms the thesis that some avowedly leftist student radicals were raised in traditional, authoritarian families. It is against this background of multiple fissures—intra-party, generational, communal, familial—revealed in contemporary West German society, that the question of continuity and change must be reviewed.

A group of recent articles post caution signs for those too eager to impose elements of continuity on the values, traditions, and aspirations of the German military from the 19th century to the present. In "The Retaming of Bellona: Prussia and the Institutionalization of the Napoleonic Legacy, 1815–1867" (*Military Affairs,* XLIV, 1980, 57–63) Dennis E. Showalter brings a new perspective to the Prussian army between Napoleon I and Napoleon III. Contrary to the common view, that the years between 1793 and 1871 were an incubation period, or "matrix," of total war, with the Prussian military elite as the agents in the unleashing of Bellona (sister of Mars), Showalter argues that these years were a time of response by the Prussian army to the forces loosed by the French Revolution. He admits that the leaders were aware of how changes in society and the complexity of military organization were calling for new kinds of leadership, but concludes that, from Clausewitz to the elder Moltke, Bellona was viewed as the servant of state policy rather than its mistress.

A significant contribution to the dissolution of prevailing myths about homogeneity and caste strictures in the higher ranks of the Prussian officer corps is made by Ulrich Trumpener in "Junkers and Others: The Rise of Commoners in the Prussian Army, 1871-1914" (*Canadian Journal of History—Annales canadiennes d'histoires,* XIV, 1979, 29-47). Basing his claims on extensive research in German archives, the author takes issue with a number of widely held views regarding the "structure and character of the Prussian army in Imperial Germany" and calls for their thorough reexamination. Challenging facile generalizations, such as Barbara Tuchman's, of German officers as cut from one of two molds, the monocled aristocrat or the red-neck, Trumpener demonstrates that the Prussian officer corps was by no means as homogeneous as is commonly assumed. On the basis of Karl Demeter's findings that aristocrats in the Prussian officer corps had been reduced from 65 per ceent in 1860 to 30 perr cent in 1913, the author nevertheless seriously doubts the conclusions drawn by other scholars from these facts. He denies that the senior positions in the Prussian army were held almost exclusively by Junkers and other blue bloods. To support his views, he provides statistical appendices, indicating significantly higher proportions of commoners in the upper ranks than previously thought. Between 1871 and 1914 approximately 20 percent of corps commanders and governors of fortresses were of commoner background, and the rate among division commanders averaged 33 per cent. Correspondingly high proportions of commoners were found in other areas, even among the section chiefs of the general staff.

Trumpener proposes further questions that need to be answered if the available information is to be interpreted meaningfully. Of these, the quantitative queries regarding appointments, promotions, patents of nobility obtained while in service, and comparative perspectives relative to other branches and jurisdictions of the military within the empire should not be too difficult to answer. Much more difficult will be the question of the extent to which the commoners in the Prussian officer corps adopted, copied, or modified the aristocratic values and modes of conduct they encountered. Without a searching documentation of these attitudes Trumpener's findings lose much of their significance, despite his demonstration of the unexpectedly large number of commoners.

According to Manfred Messerschmidt, "Militär und Schule in der Wilhelminischen Zeit" (*Militärgeschichtliche Mitteilungen,* XXIII, 1978,

51-76), the reserve officers of the Wilhelmian era did adopt the mode of conduct and value system of the active officer corps. The military sought to satisfy its manpower needs and achieve modernization of the officer corps without diluting its traditional character. Although Messerschmidt's study reveals ambiguities, fluctuations, and changes in the imperial government's position, it also establishes a rather consistent attitude on the part of the military. Despite the necessity for changes in educational requirements, the maintenance of the "nobility of spirit" (*Gesinnungsadel*), characterizing the active officer corps, clearly was given precedence; the values of an encapsuled and privileged "peace army" evidently were far more important than the needs of a prospective "war army" of enlisted men and reserve officers.

Messerschmidt perceptively shows how the pressures of modern life produced policies that oscillated between the requirements of reality and visions induced by wishful thinking. His rather sweeping title might well have been made more indicative of his study's substance by specific reference to the educational standards governing the acceptance of reserve officer candidates and the so-called *Einjährige* volunteers (serving one year only, because of their educational background), for this is his main concern. His close examination and statistical exposition of the development of these two categories during an epoch of overall army growth reveals the profound anxieties and tensions in the face of societal changes alluded to in his introduction. The strength of the forces of continuity is evident from the persistent claims made by the military leadership to influence the content and standards of the educational system, the emperor's frequent willingness to waive the requirements set by his own administration for the certification of officer candidates, and the evidently attractive status associated with the "noble calling" of the officer by the candidates and their parents. But Messerschmidt's intricate analysis of the transformed secondary school system also points to elements of change impossible for the military to overlook. The facility in modern languages more readily obtained in the *Realgymnasien* and *Oberrealschulen* than in the traditional humanistic *Gymnasien*, for example, was important to army and navy planners alike. Messerschmidt's article leaves the reader with an increased awareness of the extent of work yet to be done in this area.

A revealing comparative perspective of the military and education in Great Britain is provided in C. B. Otley's "Militarism and Militarization in the Public Schools, 1900-1972" (*British Journal of Sociology*, XXIX, 1978, 321-339). Drawing on the *Public Schools' Year Book* of 1900, 1936, and 1972, and on historical and sociological studies of public schools, the author concludes that Victorian public schools, contrary to the usual opinion, were quite military in character. They contained a "military celebratory and commendatory sub-culture," a "substantial degree" of militarism in their institutional culture, and a moderate measure of "mainly indirect militarization" in their institutional structure. Otley's paper is an invitation to systematic comparative studies.

The relationship between the military and society inevitably ties into the larger topic of politics and society. That topic is reviewed magisterially for Wilhelmian Germany by Volker Berghahn in "Politik und Gesellschaft im Wilhelminischen Deutschland" (*Neue Politische Literatur*, XXIV, 1979, 164–195). Proceeding from an analysis of the controversy over the merits of social history vis-à-vis political history, and examining in detail the voluminous literature on politics and society (including aspects of the earlier 19th century), Berghahn's study investigates the Wilhelmian *Bildungsbürgertum* (the educational and cultural elite of the middle class), imperialism, and preparations for the "grasp for world power."

His analysis of the scholarly literature reveals clearly and fairly not only the pronounced division among contemporary German historians as to the nature and meaning of the conflict between the forces of liberalism and those of authority, but also the very real division of society on that question, even if conservative attitudes carried preponderant political weight. There is a very informative exposition of recent publications on the naval building program, specifically on the relationship between the *Reichsmarineamt,* the government's Naval Office, and the *Flottenverein,* the private Navy League organized to lobby for the naval building program.

This research confirms the thesis that a good deal of "manipulation from above" was exerted to maintain at a high pitch the popular enthusiasm for a powerful navy, as well as to keep in check the "internal" and the "external" enemy. Of course, evidence of the successful manipulation of public opinion and parliamentary majorities on particular issues of armament does not, by any means, prove a conspiracy to edge the empire into the Great War. It appears from Berghahn's analysis of the literature that any continuities in the relationship between the military and society are due more to deeply rooted needs and forces than to the self-interest of conspiratorial elites. This working hypothesis, based on Berghahn's account of the plurality of forces at work in the Second Empire and of the diversity of scholarly approaches taken in unravelling them, may be tested against articles examining in more detail the relationship between the military and society during this and subsequent periods of German history.

Of immediate interest here is Geoff Eley's "Reshaping the Right: Radical Nationalism and the German Navy League, 1898-1908" (*Historical Journal*, XXI, 1978, 327-354). In what amounts to "a case study in the political tension between an old and a new right," Eley challenges the continuity thesis in German history on several points. He does not question the value of studying the coalition of capitalist interests in industry and agriculture, of examining the survival of a pre-industrial authoritarian value system, or of discussing the manipulative style of Wilhelmian politics. Nevertheless, to link such factors to Weimar and Nazi Germany by means of the continuity thesis, Eley argues, tends to obscure what is specific about fascism as one historical form of right-wing politics. By looking closely at the role presumably played by the Navy League in safeguarding the interests of the industrial-agrarian coalition, in fostering the pre-industrial authoritarian value system, and in facilitating manipulative politics toward these ends, the author shows that its efforts actually created a "fracture in the existing framework of right-wing belief." In Eley's view, the Navy League, created in 1898 and averaging 300,000 members up to 1914, radicalized conservatism and contributed to the structural changes which made fascism possible.

Eley begins with a survey of the principles on which there was agreement within the League: its nonpartisan nature and national unifying mission and function, notwithstanding an understood anti-socialist bias. Eley then addresses the issue that divided the membership. Disagreement arose over whether the Navy League program ought to be sufficiently conciliatory to accommodate the members of the Center Party or whether it should aggressively rally people of all classes and parties to the imperial ideal. Eley views the radical nationalism generated by the extreme elements dominating the leadership of the Navy League as part of a larger process. He argues that pressure groups such as the Navy League, the anti-Semitic groups, the Agrarian League, the Bavarian Peasants League, Naumann's National Social Association, and the German Mittelstand Association addressed national issues that were dealt with insufficiently by the established political parties. Eley's effort to depict the radical nationalists of the Navy League and of kindred pressure groups as combatting the class spirit of the upper and lower strata alike postulates a unity that may not be evident to all observers. His ascription to them of a "cultural optimism" and a joyful embrace of the new mechanized, urban civilization may startle those accustomed to view their generation as one of "cultural despair," but his conclusion is persuasive that the ideological reconstruction of the Right by the radical nationalists of the Navy League led to a far-reaching radicalism in the style of conservative politics. A more detailed treatment of the reaction of the military to the issues raised by the radical nationalists in their conflicts with the moderates in the Navy League would have been a welcome addition.

Of related interest is Roger Chickering, "Der 'deutsche Wehrverein' und die Reform der deutschen Armee, 1912–1914" (*Militärgeschichtliche Mitteilungen*, XXV, 1979, 7–34). Chickering's essay is particularly relevant because it clearly develops the conflict over the army's need for modernization and the social conservatism of the army leadership. The impact on this conflict by the *Deutscher Wehrverein* (DWV), the army's counterpart of the Navy League discussed in Eley's essay, reveals forces of both continuity and change: continuity in the DWV's paranoid style and appeal to plebiscites, that point to the mass movement of National Socialism, and discontinuity in how that style touched the social dominance of the governing elites. The DWV was actually founded by dissident members of the Navy League who had been forced out of that organization because their demands for further naval building programs were regarded by the government as excessive and politically untenable.

The sustained impact of the military on Wilhelmian society is shown not only by the fact that the founding members and leaders of the DWV were retired army officers, but that many active army officers also joined the organization, once it was formally established in January of 1912, and enthusiastically supported its efforts. These efforts were mainly directed at the growth and modernization of the army, to bring it up to par with the French army and to put Germany into a position to survive a two-front war. Chickering attributes the surprisingly easy passage of the two army bills of 1912 and 1913, which enlarged the army by a total of 250,000 men and 5,000 officers, to the activities of the DWV. The deeply rooted anxieties and national aspirations of German society, effectively articulated by the DWV, gave that organization an appeal beyond government, according to Chickering, that threatened the institutional balance and social structure of the empire. Focusing on the politics of armaments which increasingly dominated the years before the war, Chickering also touches on some of the key issues raised in the other essays reviewed here. By showing the preoccupation of the DWV with the advocacy of a "war army" and its indifference to, and lack of, comprehension of the effects such an enlargement would have on the traditions and fabric of the "peace army," Chickering raises the question whether the opponents of a "war army" underestimated the army's osmotic potential.

The enormous and rapid growth of the DWV, making it second to the Navy League within a year, corroborates Chickering's claim of its effect on the passage of the two army bills, but he may not have given sufficient credit to other forces at work in the Reichstag and the army command. There can be no doubt, however, that the DWV was the epitome of the *Vaterländischer Verein* (patriotic league) so characteristic of Wilhelmian politics. Chickering explores the conflicts within the establishment: the intense rivalry between army and navy, the inability of the chancellor and his cabinet to curb the war psychology, and questions about the paranoid style in German politics. His conclusions leave no doubt about the forces of continuity and change at work in the relation of the military and society.

Compared with the discerning analyses of Eley and Chickering, the poverty of East German historiography is revealed by Jürgen Lampe's "Der parlamentarische Kampf der revolutionären Sozialdemokratie gegen die Flottenvorlage von 1897" (*Militärgeschichte,* XIX, 1980, 190-196). Bound from the outset to show the continuity of "imperialist-fascist" German *Weltpolitik,* Lampe's account is an exercise in praise of the efforts by the Social Democrats in the Reichstag to defeat Tirpitz's proposal for the naval building program. The magnificent struggle against the bill by Bebel and his supporters and their shrewd awareness of the political complexities and social changes at play deserve a more differentiated treatment than that given by Lampe.

Eric J. Leed makes an important contribution to the understanding of the repercussions of the front experience, particularly on World War I volunteers, in "Class and Disillusionment in World War I" (*Journal of Modern History,* L, 1978, 680-699). In order to show what "a sociology of the knowledge gained in war" might look like, the author examines accounts by participants of encounters across class lines and the perception and definition of these encounters in the context of war. Leed focuses on the wartime experience of Franz Schauwecker, who later became one of the chief elegists of the lost *Frontgemeinschaft,* the community of the battleline, and on that of Carl Zuckmayer, a dramatist, who reacted somewhat differently. Leed also looks at the inter-class relations in the British Expeditionary Force. Predictably, experiences were interpreted along politically defined lines: soldiers with right-wing inclinations stressed the social-fusion effect of the front experience and those on the left, disillusioned over the failure to attain unity, preached class hatred even more strenuously.

As depicted by Leed, the volunteer both represented the social "no man's land" between the enlisted lower classes and the privileged officer corps, and tended to be the most perceptive recorder of the front experience, forming a revealing link between the military and the rest of society.

Leed, of course, knows that volunteers who write about their experiences are atypical and that conclusions drawn from their writings are, at best, tentative and suggestive.

Volunteers such as Schauwecker and Zuckmayer were often victimized by their enlisted comrades; the lack of appreciation of the "sacrifice" they had made in exposing themselves for the common cause produced disillusionment and efforts to compensate. Thus for some the suffering produced an expiation of guilt feelings, whereas others were aroused to an angry socialism. Still others compensated for their personal sense of isolation by depicting the entire front community as divorced from society at home, a notion exploited by nationalist agitators after the war as a powerful tool in the perpetuation of the "stab-in-the-back" legend.

Leed's article contains much food for thought in regard to the relationship between the military and Weimar society. He notes the frustration experienced by volunteers who sought some sort of social harmony and their various efforts to overcome their disillusionment. He relates the origin of contradictory postwar slogans—such as "revolutionary socialism," "new conservatism," "national socialism," and "radical conservatism"— to the "contradictory war experience" of archaic authority exalted in a milieu of proletarianization. In this regard it is particularly instructive to note the respect shown by enlisted men to aristocratic officers and their simultaneous contempt for bourgeois reserve officers. Though Leed fails to account fully for the development and persistence of this home-front dichotomy, his attempt to create a sociology of the knowledge gained through experience of the front is commendable. For a glance at encounters across the front lines as well as reactions by soldiers to their absence from home, a useful work is John Terrain's "Christmas 1914, and After" (*History Today*, XXXIX, 1979, 81–89), which examines incidents of fraternization.

The role of the volunteer in the creation of nationalist myths about the experience of the front line soldier is also discussed by George L. Mosse in "National Cemeteries and National Revival. The Cult of the Fallen Soldier in Germany" (*Journal of Contemporary History*, XIV, 1979, 1–20). Mosse considers this cult, from its early manifestation as a poetic exaltation of death during the Wars of Liberation to its apogee in Hitler's Germany, as "central to the development of nationalism." The focus of the legend of national renewal, Mosse thinks, was the volunteer who believed himself to be part of a consecrated elite, to whom fighting and dying became a sacred duty and a joyous sacrifice. He explains the durability of the myth by pointing to its function in the fulfillment of deep-seated needs.

The transcendence of the mundane and the national regeneration entailed by the cult of the fallen was co-opted by the Nazis—indeed by all fascists—and driven to an extreme.

Though Mosse's perceptive study of the "cult of the fallen" adds to his many eminent contributions, this particular essay would have benefited from a more thorough comparative analysis of the cult in other countries. He alludes only briefly to France and the more rational attitude to the cult of sacrificial death there, although he does not overlook the social impact of cemeteries and heroes' graves (*jardins funèbres*) there and elsewhere. Similarly, he does not analyze the cult in totalitarian societies of the left, particularly in Soviet Russia. Mosse's conclusion regarding the cult's effects in Germany—"undoubtedly an ever greater loss of sensitivity towards individual life and individual fate"—thus lacks force. Nevertheless, Mosse has done a valuable service by emphasizing the unique excessiveness of the cult in Germany and its role in rousing national sentiment during the Weimar years.

Perhaps most revealing for an examination of the question of continuity and change, aside from a study of the current Germanies, is the record of the Weimar Republic. For a people deeply divided politically and socially, not yet weaned from confidence in the central importance of military affairs, humiliated by defeat and condemned to settle for a glorified border patrol, the relationship with the "left-over" military was bound to be problematical. The military in the Weimar Republic, of course, must be located not only in the tiny force allowed by the treaty but also in the "diaspora" of a mighty establishment and tradition throughout a troubled society. The multitude of individual veterans and their organizations are fit subjects of study, just as much as the officers and men of the 100,000-man *Reichswehr* and *Marine* of the young republic. In addition to the interest aroused by Hindenburg and Ludendorff, particular interest is excited by the Weimar careers of Gröner, von Seeckt, and Schleicher, the "guardians" of the military tradition in Weimar Germany.

Peter Hayes examines the last of these in "A Question Mark with Epaulets? Kurt von Schleicher and Weimar Politics" (*Journal of Modern History*, LII, 1980, 34-65). Schleicher entered the army in 1900, joined the general staff in 1913, and became influential in both army and civilian politics after the war. He engaged in various intrigues that led to his appointment as war minister in 1932 in the cabinet of Franz von Papen, whom he succeeded in December of that year. Schleicher tried to create a coalition government with Hitler, whom he thought he could control, but failed and was forced by Hindenburg to resign. He was succeeded in the chancellorship by Hitler, and in 1934 Schleicher and his wife were murdered by the Nazis.

Hayes begins by reviewing the disparate contemporary characterizations of Schleicher's rise and fall. He faults both those who attribute to Schleicher a Hohenzollern authoritarianism, serving the special interests of the army, and those who depict him as intent upon stabilizing the young republic. Particular issue is joined with the interpretation of Schleicher as a man who lacked strategic sense and substantive plans. Hayes considers him to have been "neither erratic nor opportunistic" but consistent in his actions and with perceptions, methods, and objectives "much broader and more complex than those of the German Army." The emphasis on Schleicher's consistency will have to be reviewed in the light of Hayes' concluding comments.

Schleicher, according to Hayes, had learned well the lessons of Prussian and German history: a weakened country must avoid foreign policy risks and foster the recovery of its military establishment by integrating refractory groups. Bismarck's failure to curb the socialists convinced Schleicher that the oppression of genuine mass movements was counterproductive. According to Hayes, Schleicher had a constant awareness of the need to tame extremist groups by linking them to the government, and he sought "peace, economic progress, political stability, and military sufficiency." In order to clear up what might lurk behind the "Question Mark with Epaulets" of his title, Hayes places Schleicher firmly in the republican camp: not interested in restoring the monarchy but concerned with the face to be given to the new republic. In his scrupulous fairness to his subject, Hayes is reluctant to conjecture or speculate about Schleicher's ultimate vision of the new Germany. He does not attribute a modern and democratic attitude to Schleicher any more than to the many others who entered into a marriage of convenience with republicanism—the *Vernunftsrepublikaner;* but in Schleicher's attitude of moderation, his opposition in turn against extremes of the right and left alike, he sees an element of conviction unusual in those inclined to compromise.

Hayes' survey of Schleicher's Weimar career constitutes an admirable exercise in scholarship and a judicious blend of detail and synthesis. The author firmly guides the reader through the web of Weimar politics, from the crisis days of 1923–1924 through the transition from Mueller to Brüning, and to the chancellorships of von Papen and Schleicher. He is particularly aware of the options for alternative coalitions then apparently still available and is wary of the reductionist fallacy. Throughout, the reader realizes that the fortunes and the modernization of the army were indeed very much on Schleicher's mind.

If there is a criticism of substance against this article, it must come in the form of cautious suggestions. Convinced that Schleicher was "neither erratic nor opportunistic," and that he consistently pursued his larger aim of national regeneration in a peaceful and stable environment, Hayes interprets as a "Bismarckian 'strategy of alternatives'" what to other observers might well appear erratic policy, if not opportunism. The frequent shifts in Schleicher's attitude towards the Nazis, his groping for alternative coalitions, and his playing with economic philosophies clearly contrary to the traditions in which he was steeped convey the image of a man less stable than the one portrayed by Hayes. How serious was Schleicher when he declared that the army was associated "with the destinies of all strata of the people," and that it was neither the instrument of a particular faction of class nor the protector of "obsolete economic forms or unmaintainable property relations"? Did he want to maintain the army's position as supreme arbiter only in the "current crisis," or was that the ultimate and permanent priority? No doubt the politics of the disintegrating Weimar Republic called for flexibility, and the case for an underlying consistency in Schleicher's conduct is credible, but Hayes' case would be strengthened if Schleicher's ultimate ambitions were more clearly and fully defined.

The question also arises as to whether Schleicher's "ideologically unclassifiable pragmatism" might not have been really an extremely clever facade that masked his real objective. On the other hand, if he was "a bundle of atavistic impulses and rational assessments of contemporary facts," personifying "the schizophrenia of Weimar's political and social Establishment," his "consistency" appears as a zig-zag course subject to deepseated urges as well as to reason. Viewed in terms of continuity and change in the relation between the military and society, Schleicher, on balance, appears to have been an agent of continuity. Notwithstanding his rational acceptance of the republican "facts of life," he never appears to have lost sight of the guardian function assigned by history—as he understood it—to the German army relative to the rest of German society.

A strong case for continuity is made by Michael H. Kater in his examination of the claim that the armed forces were the guardians of Weimar society by maintaining domestic law and order: "Die 'Technische Nothilfe' im Spannungsfeld von Arbeiterunruhen, Unternehmerinteressen und Parteipolitik" (*Vierteljahrsheft für Zeitgeschichhte*, XXVII, 1979, 30-78). Originating in emergency measures to control the Berlin upheavals of early 1919, the *Technische Abteilungen,* forerunners of the later *Nothilfe,* consisted of army and navy regulars employed, in the main, to break strikes by providing "emergency" services. Placed under the jurisdiction of the Defense Ministry at the time of its formal establishment in October of 1919, the *Technische Nothilfe* was transferred to the authority of the Interior Ministry on November 28, 1919. Its assignment to the Interior Ministry was clearly intended to forestall conflicts over the disarmament clauses of the Versailles Treaty but, as Kater makes clear, the transfer only nominally altered the influence of the military on the *Nothilfe.* Numbering 22,430 men in January of 1920, in 1924, at the conclusion of the strikewave, the *Technische Nothilfe* had grown to almost half a million members.

Charged by decree of the Interior Ministry with securing domestic calm and order and with assisting in the reconstruction of the economy, the *Nothilfe* was to be financed by federal, state, or "self-created" funds, that is, by charging industries for protection. Outside of its Berlin headquarters, the *Technische Nothilfe* was represented in more than 1,000 state, district, and local offices and units. Its activities were justified by President Ebert as in keeping with Article 48 of the Weimar Constitution. During the heyday of its activity, from October 1, 1919 to March 31, 1925, the *Technische Nothilfe* provided over 4,000 "emergency services," mostly strikebreaking actions; it also contributed important services in providing disaster relief, flood control, and the like. Though the latter programs were featured prominently in government accounts of *Technische Nothilfe* activities, there is no doubt that its principal function was the control of labor unrest.

Kater, observing that the right to strike was not guaranteed "*expressis verbis*" in the Weimar Constitution, shows that the pseudolegal intervention of the *Technische Nothilfe* in labor strife was based on an assumed official blessing. This presumed a governmental hostility to workers that in fact was not the case. Nevertheless there was routine support of the *Nothilfe* by right-wing parliamentarians, suggesting to Kater a collusion between Reichstag members of rightist-conservative political philosophy and business interests. The *Nothilfe* functioned as the protective squad of the entrepreneurs, sharing their hatred of Communists; only 10 per cent of the membership of the *Technische Nothilfe* had working-class backgrounds.

Although their chief, the former Reserve Lieutenant Otto Lummitzsch, had exchanged his uniform for civilian garb in January of 1920, "the following years provided manifold examples of the mutual interlocking of

Technische Nothilfe activities and military interests which, up to 1926, subjected the *Technische Nothilfe* in some labor union circles to the suspicion of being, in reality, a 'fascist Freikorps.' " Based on extensive research, Kater skillfully shows the many links, including a very satisfied General von Seeckt and the complicity of a later SS leader in covering up questionable activities, which tied the *Technische Nothilfe* to the German military. Hitler never did away with the *Nothilfe*, which Kater explains by the intimate connection between the Nazi movement and the *Nothilfe* during the years of the struggle for power, the *Kampfzeit;* by their joint opposition to the right to strike; and by their mutual anti-Communism. However, since there were to be no strikes in Hitler's new Germany and he had the SS and SA to combat Communism, the duties of the *Technische Nothilfe* were redefined in October of 1933 and limited to technical services and disaster relief. Nevertheless, active cooperation in bringing about *Gleichschaltung,* the attuning of society to the Nazi doctrines, was expected to continue. During World War II the *Nothilfe*, having come fully under Himmler's command, had, among other tasks, the protection of "vital industries" against "Red" dangers, just as it had 20 years earlier.

Kater's relentless exposition of the unsavory influence exercised by the military through this paramilitary organization is punctuated by a full account of the 1928 Reichstag debate over the right to strike, which saw the democratic forces of Weimar at their best in combat with the supporters of the *Technische Nothilfe.* According to Kater, economic change—depression and rising unemployment—as much as political opposition led, in the waning years of Weimar, to the tempering of the *Nothilfe*'s anti-strike activities. On the whole, the author makes a strong case that the German military were reluctant converts to republicanism and democracy and continued to support those traditions which had dominated public affairs during the Second Empire. A fitting conclusion to this essay in continuity is found in the revival, during August, 1953, of the *Technische Nothilfe* with the new name *Technisches Hilfswerk,* under the leadership once again of Otto Lummitzsch, who retired in 1955. However, Kater carefully emphasizes that "Bonn is not Weimar." The initial fears of West-German labor unions did not materialize, and the new organization, limited to disaster relief, appears to be serving that function, though Lummitzsch himself actually had a more political, anti-Soviet concept of its activities at the time of the revival.

An East-German appraisal of efforts by the German military leadership to combat the "November Revolution" of 1918 is found in Dieter Dreetz, "Versuche der deutschen militärischen Führung zur Verhinderung oder sofortigen Niederschlagung der November Revolution 1918" (*Militär-*

geschichte, XVII, 1978, 524–533). The author stresses the relationship of the military leadership to the "counter-revolutionary" activities of para-military volunteer units such as the *Technische Nothilfe*.

Ernst Willi Hansen's "Reichswehr und Industrie: Rüstungswirtschaftliche Zusammenarbeit und wirtschaftliche Mobilmachungsvorbereitungen, 1923–1932" (*Wehrwissenschaftliche Forschungen*, XXIV, 1978, 205-245) elucidates the intimate connection between the two Weimar "power factors," the military and industry. The officer corps, still rooted in anti-modern traditions, showed an increasing awareness of the decisive role played by economic factors in the conduct of war. Describing three phases in the groundwork laid for future military mobilization—the year 1923, the period from 1924 until 1929, and the years thereafter—Hansen demonstrates how the military made public funds available to industry and facilitated rearmament without conflicting with the conditions of the Versailles treaty. The author sees the culmination of this military-industrial cooperation symbolized in Schleicher's chancellorship.

It stands to reason that much current writing on the relations of the military and society deals with Hitler and his generals. A useful overview of the political attitudes of Hitler's generals is offered by Klaus Mayer in "Wehrmachtsgeneräle in der politischen Arena" (*Neue politische Literatur*, XXIV, 1979, 85-93). Mayer attributes to the pre-1914 German officer corps the principle of "abstinence" in party politics. He describes the effects of World War I on the officers as an experience with revolutionary consequences. The generals saw the defeat as a political one, not a military one, and decided they could no longer neglect the political arena. The political roles of generals such as Beck, Guderian, von Seydlitz, Rommel, and von Kluge convey an impression of both continuity and change in the attitude of the military vis-à-vis the rest of society. Whereas the more active political engagement of many generals after World War I does indeed represent a significant change in tactics, the objectives they sought speak for a fundamental continuity of outlook. Though some of the officers were more opportunistic than others in their cooperation with Hitler, the concept of the officer corps as a privileged estate, entrusted with the guardianship of society, appears to have altered little during the Nazi period. Mayer provides an example of the "close symbiosis between the armed forces and the N.S. state" in the training of Panzer and truck drivers by the joint effort of the army and the National Socialist Motor Vehicle Corps (NSKK). This cooperation undoubtedly prevailed in many other areas. Initially a pragmatic accommodation on the part of the army, granting the Nazis a role in the military rehabilitation of Germany, this symbiosis eventually signalled a qualitative change in the relationship of the military to society which makes adherence to the continuity thesis problematical.

The presence of World War II officers in both the East German "defense forces" and the West German *Bundeswehr* again raises the question of continuity and change. While East German propaganda and restrictions of information flow do not allow a fair assessment of the question there, the issue is one widely discussed in the West. The passionate opposition to the military on the part of radical students, sketched in the introduction to this essay, must be considered a decidedly minority viewpoint in the Federal Republic. Whether the qualified support of the *Bundeswehr* by the majority includes an appreciation of *Innere Führung* (the decisive and programmatic change of the new army from the traditions of the past) cannot be determined with certainty. Media accounts of unguarded statements and actions by officers of the new army re-awaken doubts about the democratic spirit presumably governing them. But there is no question that a significant measure of change in social attitudes has occurred.

The recent periodical literature examined here reveals the determination of historians to question long-held assumptions. Though Marxist historians continue to grind their axes, their findings sometimes balance the work done in the West. The pluralism of emphases allows only tentative conclusions. The enduring determination of the German military to serve as the guardians of traditional values will surprise few; more interesting is the military's capacity to adapt to change. A fuller understanding of how the military shapes society, and vice versa, will come from comparative studies. A good start has been made in works such as those edited by Hugh Seton Watson in recent issues of the *Journal of Contemporary History* (XV, 1 and 2, 1980), surveying the adjustments to decolonization on the part of former empires, and an article by John S. Rettengill ("The Impact of Military Technology on Income Distribution" [*The Journal of Interdisciplinary History*, X, 1979, 201–255]) that uses a comparative approach to investigate the relationship between the introduction of firearms and the increased exploitation of the peasantry.

Ernest A. Menze is on the faculty of Iona College.

Journals Consulted

British Journal of Sociology • *Canadian Journal of History* • *Central European History* • *Comparative Politics* • *Geschichte in Wissenschaft und*

Unterricht • *Historical Journal* • *Historische Zeitschrift* • *History Today* • *Jahrbuch des Instituts für Geschichte* • *Journal of Contemporary History* • *Journal of Interdisciplinary History* • *Journal of Modern History* • *Militärgeschichte* • *Militärgeschichtliche Mitteilungen* • *Militärhistorische Schriftenreihe* • *Militärwissenschaft und Konfliktgeschichte* • *Military Affairs* • *Neue Politische Literatur* • *Schriftenreihe Innere Führung* • *Studien zur Militärgeschichte* • *Vierteljahrshefte für Zeitgeschichte* • *Wehrwissenschaftliche Forschungen* • *Die Zeit* • *Zeitgeschichte* • *Zeitschrift für Geschichtswissenschaft.*

ARMY, STATE, AND SOCIETY
IN THE HISTORY OF MODERN ITALY:
A REVIEW ESSAY

Benjamin F. Brown
Clara M. Lovett

An understanding of the unusual, even unique *raison d'être* of the Italian armed forces is essential to any interpretation of the relationships between the military, the state, and society in the history of modern Italy. Unlike other large powers which view their military establishment as responsible, at the very least, for the defense of national boundaries, Italy has virtually always seen her soldiers, sailors, and airmen as the guarantors of domestic peace, stability, and the social status quo. Further, Italy's armed forces include a fourth arm, the *Carabinieri*, a militarized national police force established on a French model in the Kingdom of Piedmont-Sardinia in the early 19th century.

Keeping these points in mind, it becomes much easier to evaluate Italy's military performance in wartime, the country's lack of a record of military *coups d'état* and even the obsessively secretive behavior of military leaders and institutions, which makes it rather more difficult to learn of Italy's military establishment than those in other countries.

Assumptions about the role of the military and its relationship to politics and civil society that are tenable for other Western European countries not infrequently must be reversed when interpreting the history of modern Italy. The explanation for such an unusual phenomenon is rooted in the history of the social classes that "stitched the boot" into a single political entity in the 19th century.

The Risorgimento, as the unification movement is known, was spearheaded by a small upper-class elite predominantly from or under the influence of Piedmont-Sardinia. Reformed in the 1850s under the leadership of the Piedmontese nobleman Alfonso Ferrero della Marmora, the Piedmontese army played a key role in the Lombard campaign of 1859 against Austria and in the occupation of part of the Papal States in 1860. Volunteers from every region flocked to Piedmont on the eve of the war to join in the struggle for independence and unity. In the tradition of the democratic revolutionaries Mazzini and Pisacane, many were ready to form guerrilla units like those which had fought against the Austrians in 1848. But the Piedmontese government, in agreement with liberal exiles from other regions, kept a watchful eye on their moves. Those willing to enlist in the Piedmontese army and submit to the command of its highly disciplined, monarchist officer corps were allowed to do so, while others were expelled or imprisoned.

In 1860, those who wanted the Riorgimento to be a *guerra di popolo,* an armed struggle for political and social revolution, and not merely a war of independence, found their leader in Giuseppe Garibaldi and their moment of glory in the conquest of the South. But Garibaldi's decision to surrender the conquered territories to Victor Emmanuel of Savoy, thereby closing the process of unification, crushed their last remaining hope for democratic revolution and with it the vision of a "nation-in-arms." Wary of a citizens' militia of the Swiss type, the leaders of united Italy stuck to the Piedmontese model of an army of draftees who served for a relatively long term under a professional officer corps. Indeed, for about 20 years after unification the upper ranks of both army and navy were dominated by Piedmontese officers or exiles from other regions who had received commissions in the Piedmontese army in the 1850s. But able and experienced men who had fought with Garibaldi were denied a place in the new national army.

No sooner was Italy's territorial unification completed than the new army, and to a lesser extent the navy, were entrusted with the tasks that have absorbed most of their energies and resources ever since. The first of these was the repression of domestic social unrest, especially in the rural South. The second was the civic education of young Italian males, an education intended at once to break down the linguistic and cultural barriers between regions and to foster loyalty to the Savoy dynasty and to the liberal elite. A review of current literature on the role of the military in Italian life suggests, however, that recently this state of affairs has been subjected to serious challenges which are increasingly reflected in historical interpretation and contemporary analysis.

In the last 15 years or so there has been a burst of interest in the Italian armed forces and a growing number of publications about them. Even so, these works seem few in number until they are set against the paucity of material for most of the preceding decades. United Italy may be 120 years old now, but the history of its military establishment is, at best, only emerging from infancy. This is strikingly true in comparison with Great Britain, France, Germany, and other major countries.

In his first major work, Giorgio Rochat, Italy's leading young scholar of military history, put the problem of this field of study very clearly and concisely: "The disinterest which has almost always surrounded military problems in Italy—encouraged equally from left and right, by anti-militaristic forces and by the generals themselves—continues today in Italian historiography" (*L'esercito italiano da Vittorio Veneto a Mussolini*, Bari, 1967, p. 3). Six years later, in his introductory essay to an anthology of articles on antimilitarism (*L'antimilitarismo oggi in Italia*, Turin, 1973), Rochat again commented on the obstacles to knowledge about the Italian armed forces. He candidly stated that any serious work on them is greatly hindered by the scarcity of information for the past as well as the present because of the inaccessibility of major sources. This is due, he emphasized, to a military establishment which has an exaggerated sense of the need for secrecy. This attitude has been aided over the years by the various governments of Italy as well as by the political parties of both right and left, albeit for quite diverse reasons.

Government as well as parties of the right, regarding military matters as the exclusive preserve of an undefined yet clearly understood oligarchy, have behaved as though the area were a private, even intimate matter not to be scrutinized by prying outsiders with dubious intentions, and certainly an area to be protected from the general public. The Italian left, on the other hand, with its long tradition of antimilitarism and even pacifism, has tended much more simply to damn the whole military establishment or ignore it rather than to push for any studies or investigations of it. Thus, from whichever source they came, these forces have combined to produce the same result: blocked access to virtually all archives on the Italian armed forces from the Risorgimento to the present. Rochat's warning to his readers is, therefore, well worth repeating and heeding here. In short, anyone seeking to study the Italian military establishment and its history must do so in full knowledge of the precedents of such work.

Reinforcing Rochat's assertions is the personal experience of one of the authors of this article. When preparing a major documentary series for publication with a well-established Italian publisher, a request was made of the Italian military archives in 1971 for a map of the theater of the war of 1866 in Venetia. To the astonishment of all concerned, after great delay the request was categorically rejected on the grounds that the map in question was "classified military information." There is, of course, a notable exception to the general inaccessibility of archival materials. The records of Italian military activities in World War II are available on microfilm and can be easily located through the National Archives' *Guide to the Records of the Italian Armed Forces* (Washington, D.C., 1967, 3 vols.).

Having thus set forth an unusual number of *caveats,* what is the present state of the literature on Italy's armed forces? If works in Italian are not numerous, those in English are understandably rare. It is indeed unfortunate that the British historian John Whittam's recent volume, *The Politics of the Italian Army 1861–1918* (London and Hamden, Conn., 1977) is anything but satisfactory. This work, intended to be an analytical view of the Italian army from the Risorgimento through World War I, in fact is 200 pages of anecdotal narrative with overly heavy use of biographical sketches of ministers of war and chiefs of the general staff. Any reading of Whittam's volume should be accompanied with Piero Del Negro's review article, "Army, State, and Society in the Nineteenth and Early Twentieth Century: The Italian Case" (*The Journal of Italian History,* I, 1979, 315–328), a piece worth reading in its own right for a quick but adequate understanding of the overall historical role of the army in Italy. Del Negro emphasizes the domestic, peace-keeping role of Italy's military establishment and the almost total absence of military *coups d'état* in recent times. This he attributes to the determination of Italy's socio-economic elites never to allow the military to play an independent role. On the positive side, he argues, this tradition has meant effective civilian control over the military; on the other, it has made a military career unattractive to Italy's most talented young men.

A survey of important secondary works must begin with the contributions of Piero Pieri, the dean of Italy's military historians. His *Storia militare del Risorgimento. Guerre e insurrezioni* (Turin, 1962) broke new ground in Italian military historiography as a scholarly book which departed from the official histories and also from the abundant hagiographical literature of the 19th century. Any investigation of Italy's post-unification military history must have this work as its point of departure. Particularly valuable are the chapters on the reorganization of the Piedmontese army in the 1850s. An understanding of the social and strategic thinking of the professionals in the Piedmontese army is, in fact, essential to evaluate the military institutions and practices of united Italy. Also useful to the same end is Carlo Pischedda's article, "L'esercito piemontese: aspetti politici e sociali" (in *Problemi dell'unificazione italiana,* Modena, 1963, 7–101). Both works describe the dilemma of the Piedmontese ruling class at mid-19th century. Inclined by tradition and preference to follow the French example, the Piedmontese nevertheless found that the army of Napoleon III did not provide a model they could imitate. In the midst of a major drive for economic and cultural modernization, they needed something closer to the Prussian *Landwehr,* in which all able-bodied males served for a short time. Yet the Piedmontese government balked at the idea that lower-class men might be given arms and be taught how to use them. The result was a compromise—a Piedmontese, and later on an Italian army which incorporated some features of both systems.

Another valuable work by Pieri is his *Le forze armate nell'età della Destra* (Milan, 1962) which spans roughly the years 1861 to 1876, but which encompasses the best single account of the founding of the Italian army and navy. Supplementing Pieri's other volume, this account describes the formation of a national army for Italy around the nucleus of that of Piedmont-Sardinia and the utilization in part of the current French and Prussian models. A significant section of the book is composed of such items as the bills presented to Parliament for the structuring of the armed forces, as well as other significant contemporary documents. The work of La Marmora, Ricotti-Magnani and Fanti, the three generals who created the Italian army, is ably described and documented. The brief section on the creation of the navy by the merger of the Piedmontese and Neapolitan fleets is also instructive. With regard to the army, only one account takes the story past World War I and into, but not through, the fascist era: G. Rochat's previously cited *L'esercito italiano.* This and a subsequent volume by the same author on the background of the Ethiopian campaign (*Militari e politici nella preparazione della campagna d'Etiopia,* Milan, 1971) make up virtually all the scholarly literature on the interwar years. These two volumes together, however, provide most useful insights into the role of the military in the rise and consolidation of the fascist regime. Above all, they challenge the widely held view that the Italian army and navy remained monarchist in spirit and that they were reluctant collaborators in the building of Mussolini's empire. If it is undoubtedly true that the strongest support for the regime came from the air force, Rochat's work nonetheless shows that wars of conquest, justified by the fascist ethos, were a welcome change of pace even for tradition-bound army and navy officers.

Summary observations on the general coverage of the Italian armed forces can only point up the highly uneven coverage of the various arms within the sparse literature that does exist. If the army has fared, at best, adequately, the navy has received very little attention, particularly in view of its importance (the world's fourth largest) before World War I. The air force is wholly without a history despite the fact that Italy was the first country to be bombed from the air (Venice by balloon in 1866), the first to use mechanized aircraft in warfare (Libya, 1912), and the home of the founder of the concept of strategic air bombardment (Giulio Douhet).

Publications concerning the Italian armed forces since World War II tend to fall into two uneven categories. There are a few solid and reliable factual works such as Nico Arena's *L'aeronautica nazionale repubblicana, 1943–45* (Modena, 1974, 2 vols.) which is a detailed technical account, well illustrated, of the air force of Mussolini's rump Republic of Salò. Although there is ample glorification of Italian airmen, fascist or not, the volume is useful for its broad documentation of Italian-German military ties.

In the same category is Enea Cerquetti's general work on *Le forze armate italiane dal 1945 al 1975* (Milan, 1975). Despite a clear leftist point of view, this work is still the most useful general treatment of the subject for the recent past. Highly detailed and rather technical, it recounts the use of the Italian armed forces as an instrument of American policy. Once the defender of the domestic status quo and the protector of those in power, the Italian military establishment, Cerquetti argues, is now the principal guarantor of NATO in the Mediterranean. Its historic role has expanded without changing in character.

Providing a bridge of sorts into the second category of works done since 1945—those of a polemical nature focusing on NATO and atomic arms policy—is a brief and very useful analysis of Italian foreign policy vis-à-vis the U.S. and the Atlantic Alliance: Primo Vannicelli, *Italy, NATO and the European Community: The Interplay of Foreign Policy and Domestic Politics* (Cambridge, Mass., 1974). Although not directed at the Italian military establishment as such, this volume is crucial to anyone who would understand the background and complexities of Italy's postwar love/hate relationship with NATO.

Finally, the larger category of publications on the military since World War II tends to be somewhat polemical and inspired by a pacifist and leftist view. Perhaps the most useful work in this category is a curious dual volume entitled *Che fare della NATO? Atti del Convegno di Politica* (Florence, 1967). The first 110 pages of this volume reproduce the statements of participants in a Florentine conference of September, 1967 organized by the magazine *Politica*. The speakers, Christian Democrats and Socialists, gathered to examine NATO at a distance of 20 years and to determine whether or not they found it outdated. The second part of the volume, *Le forze politiche italiane e l'adesione al Patto atlantico* by Giovanni di

Capua, is a very enlightening and highly detailed account of Italy's curious and slightly oblique entry into NATO.

Finally, for diverse views of Italians on nuclear policy and pacifism, two interesting works can be cited. Achille Albonetti's *L'Italia e l'atomica* (Faenza, 1976) was published at the author's expense. He asserts the anti-nuclear left blocked this and other efforts to discuss Italy's nuclear policy and argues that for 50 years the left has been so occupied with its pacifism that it has neglected broad policy issues. The result, shown here with the use of documents from various sources, has been a policy worked out semi-secretly and haphazardly by military men and technocrats with little reference to democratic legal processes.

The previously cited collection of essays, *L'antimilitarismo oggi in Italia,* edited by G. Rochat, covers an issue prevalent in Italian society for generations and still strong today. Rochat begins with an excellent essay on the Italian military today and then presents more than 100 selections illustrative of antimilitarism in Italy since the 1890s. Giving particular attention to the conscientious-objection movement, Rochat points out that Italian antimilitarism has long run in two broad strains: that of labor within a Marxist tradition and the non-violent tradition of Christian humanitarians. Both of these volumes, though edited by, respectively, a technocrat of international repute and a highly regarded historian, are good preparation for reading the often markedly polemical but provocative contemporary critiques of the military in Italian life.

In his *Bianço, rosso e grigioverde; Struttura e ideologia delle forze armate italiane* (Verona, 1974) Giulio Massobrio, a historian of 20th-century Italy and a critic of existing military-institutions, summarizes the attitude of young Italian intellectuals vis-à-vis the ongoing transformation of Italian culture and society: "Unlike our predecessors, after scores of generations we are finally beginning to realize that our survival does not depend upon the preservation of certain traditional values but rather upon their elimination within the shortest possible time" (p. 9). One of the "traditional values" that is most obviously under attack by men of Massobrio's generation is the belief (some would say the myth) that the armed forces, as presently organized, are a shield against foreign enemies and a school of discipline, patriotism, and civic virtue.

The historical literature reviewed above, especially the recent scholarly works by Rochat, make it clear enough that the Italian armed forces often have lacked both offensive and defensive capabilities vis-à-vis foreign enemies, but have functioned rather effectively as an instrument of social control. Taking this as a given, in the last decade several authors have undertaken to explore how such control is exercised and how it can be effectively weakened and subverted. The sheer number of works published on this topic in the 1970s represents a sharp departure from the years of indifference to and neglect of things military.

One such work, Angelo D'Orsi's *La macchina militare* (Milan, 1971), ends with the statement that "to deal with the military question today is to focus on the social forces and structures that are holding up Italian society" (p. 238). D'Orsi points out that most critics of the existing system are on the left and that their objectives since the 1940s have been to democratize the armed forces; to narrow the class cleavage between soldiers and officers; to reform disciplinary practices that are nearly a century old; and to change the definition of "military secret," which now protects incompetence, corruption, and abuses of power more than it protects the national security. Sympathetic to these objectives, D'Orsi nevertheless admits that the advocates of change lack appropriate role models. The Risorgimento ideal of a "nation-in-arms" is obviously inappropriate to a military establishment which, like all others in industrialized countries, depends on highly skilled technical personnel to function effectively in the event of war. Equally irrelevant role models are the revolutionary "people's armies" of the Cuban or Chinese type.

The anonymous author of *Da quando son partito militare* (Rome, 1973), a collection of testimonials by "proletarians in uniform," discusses some of the reasons why a military establishment that is almost universally criticized and not infrequently ridiculed by both Italians and foreigners nevertheless has proved remarkably impervious to reform. The existing army of draftees, this author argues, is top-heavy, poorly armed, and generally inefficient. Yet it is highly "functional" with regard to Italy's socio-economic institutions. By keeping over 500,000 men in uniform at any given time (of whom about 85,000 are in the *Arma dei carabinieri*), the armed forces provide an economic safety valve that relieves unemployment.

In addition to this economic function, the military continues to perform time-honored educational and police functions. By helping preserve the status quo, however, the armed forces are not serving the interests of a separate and distinct military elite but rather those of the political ruling classes generally. Again, this author emphasizes that Italy's military leaders "have never provided a credible alternative to the policies of the civilian elites; the Joint Chiefs of Staff themselves represent political forces and personalities more than they do specific sections of the military establishment" (p. 14).

Ironically, the lack of a distinct "military viewpoint" which has been characteristic of Italian life since the unification is not an indication of a tradition of civilian control over the military. In a useful collection of essays, *Il potere militare in Italia* (Bari, 1971), Fabrizio De Benedetto, Giorgio Rochat and others explore this paradox. Their conclusion is that institutional controls over the military have always been weak and ineffective. The absence of military *coups d'état*, then, must be viewed as a result of the highly class-bound recruitment to the military academies, whose graduates have held political opinions very similar to those of civilian elites. This atmosphere of consensus began to change in the 1960s with the advent to power of left-wing Christian Democrats and Socialists. However, the possibility of meaningful parliamentary scrutiny of the armed forces that was then opened has been undermined, these authors argue, by the increasing importance and near autonomy of the technocratic elements.

Except for this volume, which contains contributions by noted historians, sociologists, and economists, discussions of the "failed democratization" of Italy's armed forces and of their inability to provide for the country's defense are most often found in non-scholarly books by journalists on the far left of the political spectrum. Their chief target is the Italian Communist Party (PCI), accused of betraying the antimilitarist tradition of its socialist ancestors and of supporting NATO. These criticisms at first sight seem outrageous because the PCI in the 1940s and 1950s led not only the campaign against Italy's participation in NATO but also the fight to restructure the armed forces. Yet to some extent the criticisms are justified, reflecting as they do an important shift in the PCI's position on "the military question," away from a quasi-pacifist, dogmatic opposition to all NATO-related matters, toward constructive criticism of military spending, training, and secrecy. The shift may ultimately produce the political will and the parliamentary majority needed to turn the cumbersome Italian military machine from an instrument of class hegemony (in the Gramscian sense), and even of repression, into the defense establishment it has historically claimed to be.

Benjamin F. Brown is a member of The Institute for Research in History. Clara M. Lovett, also a member of The Institute for Research in History, is on the faculty of Baruch College, The City University of New York.

Journals Consulted

Il Carabiniere • Il Ponte • Journal of Italian History • Journal of Modern History • Nuova rivista storica • Rassegna storica del Risorgimento • Rivista militare • Storia contemporanea • Storia e politica.

THE RUSSIAN MILITARY (1700-1917): SOCIAL AND ECONOMIC ASPECTS

Walter M. Pintner

Although the central importance of military institutions in Imperial Russia is frequently mentioned, historians, whether western or Soviet, have devoted very little attention to Russian military history. For western historians the explanation lies in the course of the field's development since World War II. Initially, research concentrated on intellectual history and the origins of Russian radicalism, areas in which interest was high and the primary sources most easily available. Since the late 1950s, as the number of scholars in the field has grown and archival research in the Soviet Union has become possible, the social, economic, and political institutions of Imperial Russia have come under serious scrutiny. Cities, merchants, churchmen, lawyers, bureaucrats, radicals and conservatives, central and local government, not to mention the ever present peasants and nobles, have all received serious scrutiny. Military institutions, however, with the exception of the work of Richard Hellie, *Enserfment and Military Change in Muscovy* (Chicago, 1971), on the pre-Petrine army and of John Curtiss, *The Russian Army Under Nicholas I, 1825-1855* (Durham, 1965), on the army under Nicholas I (Tsar 1825-1855), still await careful study. The explanation is probably that civilian historians are reluctant to embark on a topic that seemingly involves a whole new range of unfamiliar technical questions, while military men concerned with history are naturally oriented to the Soviet period.

It is perhaps surprising that the situation is almost exactly the same in the Soviet Union. Until very recently Soviet scholars were primarily concerned with the origins of the revolutionary movement, the development of the working class, and the condition of the peasantry. The institutions of the old regime, including the military, have come to enjoy serious examination only in the past decade or so. Just as in the West, there seems to be a sharp division between a present-oriented group of professional military historians and a very few civilian historians who deal with pre-revolutionary military history (notably L. G. Beskrovnyi and, at times, P.

A. Zaionchkovskii). The *Voenno-istoricheskii zhurnal* (*Journal of Military History*), published by the Ministry of Defense, is almost exclusively concerned with post-1917 military history (particularly World War II). Less than five per cent of recent items deal with the pre-revolutionary period, and those are usually very brief "communications from readers," not full-fledged articles. This small number of contributions, in turn, consists primarily of traditional military history, dealing with strategy, tactics, and leadership. Nevertheless, historians, like nature, abhor a vacuum and in recent years both Soviet and western scholars have begun to give serious consideration to important aspects of the social and economic history of Imperial Russian military institutions.

The first step in the social analysis of a group of people is to find out who they are in terms of as many variables as possible. At opposite ends of the chronological spectrum, the task has been begun by a Soviet and an American, with the publication in 1973 of M. D. Rabinovich's "Sotsial'noe proiskhozhdenie i imushchestvennoe polozhenie ofitserov reguliarnoi russkoi armii v kontse severnoi voiny" ("The Social Origin and Property Holding of Officers in the Regular Russian Army at the End of the Northern War" [*Rossiia v period reform Petra I*, Moscow, 1973, 133–171]) and Peter Kenez's "A Profile of the Pre-revolutionary Officer Corps" (*California Slavic Studies*, VII, 1973, 121–158). Although there are profound differences between the early 18th century and the late 19th, the two articles together provide a sense of development. Kenez points to the end of noble predominance in the officer corps and calls it a "middle class occupation" on the eve of the Revolution. Nevertheless, Rabinovich shows us that in the 1720s by no means all officers were noble and that many of the nobles were career officers with little or no land. What happened in the intervening 150 years remains to be fully examined. Was the nobility ever as predominant in the officer corps as is usually assumed?

One sub-group of the officer corps is examined by Bruce W. Lincoln in "A Re-examination of Some Historical Stereotypes: An Analysis of the Career Patterns and Backgrounds of the Decembrists" (*Jahrbücher für Geschichte Osteuropas*, XXIV, 1976, 357–368). Lincoln provides a detailed examination of the backgrounds and careers of the 300-odd officers who were involved in the groups connected with the abortive attempt at a *coup d'état* in December, 1825: The Northern Society, The Southern Society, and the Society of United Slavs. He does not dispute the traditional view that the movement was drawn from the upper levels of the nobility, but he does show that the Northern Society had the greatest number of elite members and the Society of United Slavs the least. His most interesting finding is that only a small proportion (10 to 20 per cent) of the men involved had actually visited western Europe either on military duty in the Napoleonic era or as private travelers. The general view has always been that direct contact with the West was one of the prime causes of discontent over conditions in Russia.

Matitiahu Mayzel studies another group of officers in "The Formation of the Russian General Staff, 1880-1917: A Social Study (*Cahiers du monde russe et sovietique*, XVI, 1975, 297-321). Mayzel makes a major contribution with his discussion of how, in the latter 19th century, the vigorous selection procedures for admission to the General Staff Academy and the General Staff itself created an "elite of merit" that replaced the old-guard officer elite based on family connections and wealth. The contrast between this top two per cent of the officer corps and the poorly qualified and poorly paid mass that Kenez describes is striking. Why the "*Genshtabistsy,*" who had a virtual monopoly on high command positions in World War I, were so unsuccessful militarily has yet to be explained. Was their intense training inadequate in some respect, or were the problems they faced simply too great to be dealt with successfully? A concrete example of the work of the General Staff officers is provided by A. Ageev in "Ofitsery russkogo generalnogo shtaba ob opyte russko-iaponskoi voiny, 1904-05"—"Officers of the Russian General Staff on the Experience of the Russo-Japanese War, 1904-05"—(*Voenno-istoricheskii zhurnal*, VIII, 1975, 99-104). The report prepared by the staff officers was extremely critical of the performance of the Russian army and did not hesitate to comment negatively on the performance of the high command itself. The *Genshtabistsy* clearly enjoyed a privileged position.

The rank and file of the army has thus far received less attention than the officer corps. Iu. F. Prudnikov's "K voprosu komplektovaniia rossiskoi armiia (1794-1796 gg.)—"Regarding the Question of Recruitment for the Russian Army (1794-1796)"—(*Vestnik moskovskogo universiteta, seriia istorii*, IV, 1970, 15-26) describes the difficulties experienced in filling recruit levies, but provides very limited data on the types of men recruited or even the nature of the recruitment process itself. Indeed the whole subject of recruitment both before and after the reforms of 1874, which instituted short-term universal military service and a reserve system to replace the standing army of long-term peasant conscripts, remains an area of enormous importance that has yet to be thoroughly studied. The only reasonably recent work that deals with the social composition of the enlisted forces appears to be L. G. Protasov's "Klassovyi sostav soldat russkoi armii pered okitabrem"—"The Class Composition of the Soldiers

of the Russian Army before October''—(*Istoriia SSSR,* 1, 1977, 33-48).
Protasov provides a useful list of earlier studies of the problem, most of
which deal with sailors rather than soldiers. The data are difficult to work
with, but the article makes an important contribution in showing that the
proportion of peasants among the soldiers was perhaps a bit lower (63 to 66
per cent) and the literacy rate higher (71 per cent) than has generally been
assumed.

A much broader view of the life of the enlisted man in the pre-
revolutionary army is taken by John Bushnell in "Peasants in Uniform:
The Tsarist Army as a Peasant Society" (*Journal of Social History,* XIII,
1980, 565-576). The argument is that the military reforms of 1874 which
established general conscription and relatively short-term service had a
very limited role in introducing the peasant to the ways of the modern
world. Life in the army, after a short period of basic training, was very
similar to life in the village. Bushnell's evidence for this surprising conclusion is impressive. Between 1880 and 1902 attempts to introduce literacy
were abandoned, and even more important much of the army's enlisted
manpower was diverted to "economic duties": manufacturing clothing and
equipment, raising food, or even doing contract labor for private firms or
municipalities. Relations between officers and men were reminiscent of
those between estate owners and peasants. Officers were remote and dealt
with their men almost exclusively through non-commissioned officers, just
as the estate owners dealt with the hired hands.

Despite Bushnell's provocative study, the impact of the military reforms
of 1874 remains a subject much in need of careful study. The reform era
itself has received somewhat more attention. The need for improvements in
the navy and the role of Grand Duke Konstantine Nikolaevich in imple-
menting them is examined by Jacob Kipp, "Consequences of Defeat:
Modernizing the Russian Navy, 1856-1863" (*Jahrbücher für Geschichte
Osteuropas,* XX, 1972, 210-225) and "Charisma, Crisis and the Genesis
of Reform: The Konstantinovtsy and Russian Naval Modernization:
1853-1858" (International Commission for Military History, *ACTA* 2,
Washington, 1975, 85-96); and by Aurele J. Violette, "The Grand Duke
Konstantine Nikolaevich and the Reform of Naval Administration, 1855-
1870" (*Slavonic and East European Review,* LII, 1974, 584-601), "Re-
forms of Naval Officer Education in Russia During the Reign of Alexander
II" (*European Studies Review,* VI, 1976, 427-448), and "Judicial Reforms in the Russian Navy During the 'Era of Great Reforms': The Reform
Act of 1867 and the Abolition of Corporal Punishment" (*Slavonic and
East European Review,* LVI, 1978, 586-603). These articles demonstrate

that reforms in the navy proceeded more rapidly than in the army, in part because it was directly under the jurisdiction of Konstantine Nikolaevich, the Tsar's brother, but also because it was much smaller. Changing the navy did not have the massive implications for society as a whole that any major innovation in the army entailed. That the Russian government was not monolithic is well illustrated by Kipp (1975) where he points out that the navy under Konstantine Nikolaevich was used as a proving ground for more extensive reforms contemplated elsewhere by some officials, as in the case of the naval "artisan-serfs" who were freed in 1858, three years before the general emancipation proclamation.

In 1966 Alfred Rieber proposed that the emancipation of the serfs was closely linked to Alexander II's (1855-1881) desire to introduce a system of universal military conscription, to permit the reduction of the standing army and the development of a large trained reserve force. Such a system was incompatible with serfdom because of the long-established principle that once a peasant entered the army he ceased to be a serf, and, should he survive his 25-year term, would not be forced to return to his master. Few did survive, so no serious social problems arose. However, with short-term service involving a large proportion of the peasant population, the situation would be entirely different and potentially very dangerous for the stability of rural areas. Rieber's argument has received widespread and favorable attention, but it is far from universally accepted. Dietrich Beyrau, in "Von der Niederlage zur Agrarreform: Leigeigenschaft und Militärverassung in Russland nach 1855" (*Jahrbücher für Geschichte Osteuropas,* XXIII, 1975, 191-222), discusses the relationship between the desire to introduce a military reserve system and general conscription to the abolition of serfdom. He describes the measures taken to expand the reserve force even before the general reform of 1874. Beyrau is sympathetic to the "Rieber thesis," but sees no specific evidence for attributing that motivation to Alexander himself.

It was not only in the period of the "Great Reforms" that military institutions and high politics were interrelated, but only in the work of John L. H. Keep is this crucial subject examined. In one of the few recent articles that deals with the 18th century, he discusses the crucial interrelationship between the security apparatus of the state and the influential, strategically located, guards regiments. "The Secret Chancellery, the Guards and the Dynastic Crisis of 1740-1741" (*Forschungen zur Osteuropäischen Geschichte,* XXV, 1978, 169-193) points out that the Guards were both the immediate source of support for the monarchs and their favored instruments, and at the same time a potential danger should their loyalty waiver; therefore they were subject to the scrutiny of the Secret Chancellery. Keep argues that the deposition of Ivan VI (1740–1741) and the accession of Elizabeth 1741–1762 was made possible by the ambiguous attitude of the Secret Chancellery headed by Major-General of the Guards, A. I. Ushakov, which uncovered disloyalty among guardsmen, but failed to act against it in a decisive manner. In the latter 18th century the guards continued to play a political role, but one separate from the state security apparatus.

Keep has pursued his work on the interrelationship of the political and social institutions in three other articles. In "Paul I and the Militarization of Government" (*Paul I: A Reassessment of his Life and Reign,* edited by Hugh Ragsdale, Pittsburgh, 1979, 91–103) he argues that Paul's reign (1796–1801) had a three-fold impact on the governmental process: it demarcated the lines between civilian and military authority more clearly than in the past; shifted the locus of executive power away from the aristocratic elite to professional administrators; and militarized the ethos of public service. Unfortunately many of the positive features of these changes, such as the clear division of authority, were discarded in the reaction against Pauline measures after his murder, but negative features, such as the indifference to legality, seem to have been preserved throughout the first half of the 19th century.

"The Russian Army's Response to the French Revolution" (*Jahrbücher für Geschichte Osteuropas,* forthcoming) includes an intriguing demonstration of the connection between the "national school" of Russian military thought which looked back with pride to the tradition of Suvorov and rejected the "Prussian school" associated with the unpopular Paul I, and the attitudes of the Decembrist officers who made the first attempt to change the Russian political system in their abortive *coup d'état* in 1825. In that analysis Keep uses memoirs to good effect, a source that he will consider at length in "From the Pistol to the Pen: The Military Memoir as a Source on Russian Social History" (*Cahiers du monde russe et sovietique,* forthcoming).

The Decembrist movement is, of course, the subject of an extensive Soviet literature but the only recent article which relates it to the social aspects of military history is I. Miroshnikov's note, "Voennyi poseleniia v planakh dekabristov"—"The Military Colonies in the Plans of the Decembrists"—(*Voenno-istoricheskii zhurnal,* I, 1977, 97–99). The military colonies were the Imperial regime's ambitious but unpopular and ultimately unsuccessful attempt to transform whole villages of state-owned peasants into military units. Miroshnikov argues that the aristocratic Decembrists saw the discontent in these settlements as a source of support for their attempt at revolution. It is a significant conclusion since upperclass Russians generally feared peasant revolt, whatever their views on other matters. The short note, however, needs further documentation.

Except for the work on the navy in the era of reforms, mentioned above, military administration has received almost no attention. Yet some ancillary administrative fields have been studied. In the last decade of Nicholas I's reign there was some progress in the direction of a more formally defined and professional system of military justice, according to John P. Le Donne in "The Administration of Military Justice under Nicholas I" (*Cahiers du monde russe et sovietique*, XIII, 1972, 180-191). Schools were established to train military legal officials, but the ability of the Tsar to override formal legal authority and procedures perpetuated a major element of illegality, despite the progress made. Basil Haigh deals with an entirely different aspect of administration in his "Design for a Medical Service: Peter the Great's Admiralty Regulation, 1722" (*Medical History*, XIX, 1975, 129-146). The statutes were based on French and Dutch sources and dealt with dockyard workers, not sailors. Russia began the 18th century with an up-to-date plan for medical service in at least one area. Haigh does not discuss the implementation of the regulations.

Problems of supply, finances, and the development of military-related industry are also largely ignored in recent periodical literature. A 1961 article by V. N. Avtokratov, "Pervye kommissariatskie organy russkoi reguliarnoi armii (1700-1710 gg.)"—"The First Commissariat Agencies of the Regular Russian Army"—(*Istoricheskie zapiski*, LXVIII, 1961, 163-188) describes Peter's initial attempts to organize finance and supply in the most difficult years of the Great Northern War, but there has been nothing to continue the discussion of organization for the succeeding 200 years. Heinz Muller-Dietz gives us a useful view of the kind of personnel problems that faced Russian commanders in "Die wirtschaftliche Verhältnisse Russischer Truppenartzte um 1770" (*Forschungen zur Osteuropaischen Geschichte*, XXV, 1978, 271-282). Pay was low and the death rate high (from diseases), conditions that certainly applied to other hard-to-replace specialists.

A recent article by the dean of Soviet military historians, L. G. Beskrovnyi, "Proizvodstvo vooruzheniia i boepripasov dlia armii v Rossii v period imperializma (1898-1917 g.)"—"The Production of Weapons and Ammunition for the Army in Russia in the Period of Imperialism (1898-1917)"—(*Istoricheskie zapiski*, XCIX, 1977, 88-139) gives extensive data on Russian production of the major types of weapons and ammunition and also discusses the extent to which Russia's military leaders foresaw the nature of the European war that seemed inevitable in the first decade of the 19th century. According to Beskrovnyi a number of important Russian military thinkers (Gulevich, Leer, Mikhnevich, and Neznamov) anticipated the mass character of the conflict, but the General Staff (like those in the West) assumed that for that very reason the war would be of short duration.

In dealing with the thought of N. P. Mikhnevich, A. Ageev also notes that Mikhnevich (1849-1927) anticipated the impact of technology and mass mobilization of resources on warfare, and that Mikhnevich even argued that the coming war would be one of position, "Voenno-teoreticheskie vzgliady N. P. Mikhnevicha"—"The Military-Theoretical Views of N. P. Mikhnevich"—(*Voenno-istoricheskii zhurnal*, I, 1975, 90-95). Finally, V. V. Mavrodin and P. Sh. Sot have published a useful bibliographical essay on Russian rifles, showing that a considerable literature exists on the technology and production of these weapons. "Sovetskaia istoriografiia otechestvennogo strelkovogo oruzhiia XIX - nachale XX v."—"Soviet Historiography of Domestic Rifled Weapons, 19th through the Beginning of the 20th Century"—(*Vestnik Lenigradskogo Universiteta*, XIV, 1976, 45-51).

Imperial Russia was a multi-national empire but the role of minority groups in the military has been almost entirely ignored. The only substantial exception is in the case of the Cossacks, not a national or religious minority, but a group of frontiersmen with a very distinct social and political tradition and an important specialized role in the Russian military system. The Imperial government's attempts to cope with the social and military problems of the steppe frontier are discussed by Bruce W. Menning in a series of recent and forthcoming articles. In "Military Institutions and the Steppe Frontier in Imperial Russia, 1700-1861" (International Commission for Military History, *ACTA*, 1980) he argues that scant population and sparse resources made supply with standard 18th-century techniques impossible. Speed was essential if the army was not to starve or succumb to disease before accomplishing its aims, a plausible explanation, he asserts, for the Russian propensity to storm fortresses rather than lay siege. Traditional European linear tactics were adjusted to deal with the Turkish Cavalry.

However, the transfer of military flexibility learned on the southern frontier to the main European theatres of war was slow and limited, according to another article, "G. A. Potemkin and A. I. Chernyshev: Two Dimensions of Reform and the Military Frontier in Imperial Russia" (Consortium on Revolutionary Europe, *Proceedings,* 1980). The most important social development was the integration of the formerly autonomous population of Cossack freebooters into the Russian army as a special cavalry force that largely supported itself in exchange for economic privileges in its home territory. Indeed so successful was the Imperial program that within a few generations the independent Cossack captains were transformed into loyal members of the Russian service nobility, and the rank-and-file Cossacks sank to a status perilously close to enserfment: "The Emergence of a Military-Administrative Elite in the Don Cossack Land, 1708-1836" (Walter M. Pintner and Don K. Rowney, eds., *Russian Officialdom: The Bureaucratization of Russian Society from the Seventeenth to the Twentieth Century,* New York, 1980, 130-161). The process of integration and social differentiation, although rapid, was not without some difficulties, such as the protests against non-Cossack settlement that Menning discusses in "Cossacks Against Colonization: Mutiny in the Don" (Bela K. Kiraly and Gunther Rothenberg, eds., *War and Society in East Central Europe During the 18th and 19th Centuries,* vol. II, New York, 1980). Philip Longworth surveys the entire course of the social transformation of the Cossacks from the 17th to the 19th century in "The Transformation of Cossackdom 1650-1850" (Bela K. Kiraly and Gunther Rothenberg, eds, *War and Society in East Central Europe During the 18th and 19th Centuries,* vol. I, New York, 1979, 393-407). Finally, Robert H. McNeal examines the last phase of Cossack history in "The Reform of Cossack Military Service in the Reign of Alexander II" (*ibid,* 411-421). Paralleling the general military reforms of 1874, Cossack service was regularized, and although it was more burdensome than that imposed on the general population, it maintained the Cossack community's separate identity and traditions, certainly one reason that these once independent frontiersmen ended up as the last bulwark of the autocracy.

To date, the social and economic aspects of Russia's military effort seem to be too new a field to have evoked any body of general interpretive literature. Perhaps the basis for such speculations is as yet too thin. Richard Hellie's discussion of the army of Peter the Great, "The Petrine Army: Continuity, Change, and Impact" (*Canadian-American Slavic Studies,* VIII, 1974, 237-253) argues that, in large measure, the changes introduced by Peter were extensions and developments of the major innovations already well under way in the reign of his father, Alexis Mikhailovich (1645-1676), who undertook the basic shift from a gentry cavalry militia to a standing infantry force of conscripted peasants trained by professional officers. Even the link between rank and effective service that is so often attributed to Peter is assigned to the 17th century by Hellie. P. A. Zaion-chkovskii's recent work on the late 19th century army, *Samoderzhavie i russkaia armiia na rubezhe XIX–XX stoletii* (*The Autocracy and the Russian Army at the Turn of the 19th to the 20th Centuries*, Moscow, 1973) is discussed in a review article by Peter Kenez, "Autocracy and the Russian Army" (*Russian Review*, XIII, 1974, 201–205). Kenez credits the author with another major contribution to the study of old-regime Russia, citing particularly the social profiles of the officer corps and the perceptive discussion of the negative role of leadership by members of the royal family.

This survey of recent literature demonstates that military institutions of all sorts in imperial Russia are fertile for further study. There has been fairly extensive work on certain specialized topics, the officer corps, the Cossacks, the naval reforms, but the fundamental aspects of the army, the main military force, such as the character and training of the rank and file soldiers, the whole process of recruitment, the basic problems of supply and transport, the mobilization of fiscal and industrial resources for military use have been approached by very few of the authors surveyed. Russia, after all, became a great power in the course of the 18th century. Its efforts to maintain that position in the 19th were a major cause of the collapse of the old regime. We still have much to learn about the military institutions that contributed so much to both the successes and failures.

Walter M. Pintner is on the faculty of Cornell University.

Journals Consulted

Cahiers du monde russe et soviétique • *California Slavic Studies* • *Canadian Slavonic Papers* • *Canadian-American Slavic Studies* • *Forschungen zur Osteuropäischen Geschichte* • *Istoricheskie zapiski* • *Istoriia SSSR* • *Jahbücher für Geschichte Osteuropas* • *Oxford Slavic Papers* • *Russian History* • *Russian Review* • *Slavic Review* • *Slavonic and East European Review* • *Trudy po russkoi i slavianskoi filologii* (Tartu) • *Vestnik Leningradskogo Universiteta* • *Vestnik Moskovskogo Universiteta* • *Voenno-istoricheskii zhurnal* • *Voprosii istorii.*

MILITARISM AND MILITARIZATION
IN MODERN CHINESE HISTORY

David Strand
Ming K. Chan

Historians of China rarely write conventional military history which is exclusively concerned with strategy, tactics, and what happens on the battlefield. But they often write about the causes, consequences and context of military campaigns and battles. Most military action in modern Chinese history has taken place on Chinese soil in the form of rebellions, *coups d'état,* civil wars, revolution and foreign invasion. The impact of warfare on civil society has been so immediate and intense that any attempt to compartmentalize military history as a chronicle of battles would seem one dimensional.

In the 18th century, on the eve of the modern era, Chinese society was substantially at peace. Military energies were spent in waging border wars and not in suppressing internal rebellion or resisting foreign invaders. With the aid of Chinese armies and logistics support, the Manchu founders of the Ch'ing dynasty (1644-1912) had doubled the size of the empire. The Ch'ing used a variety of military strategies to defend these long borders including conquest and control of border peoples, long-range punitive expeditions and temporary mobilization of local communities.

Imperial borders were often marked, not by administrative or natural boundaries, but by the shifting position of subject peoples. As Henry Serruys shows in the case of the Caqar people of Mongolia, the Manchus aggressively managed these human borders. The Ch'ing dynasty used a combination of diplomacy and coercion to deprive the Caqar of the aristocracy which led them in battle. The leaderless tribes were then organized into Manchu style "banner" military units which were quite alien to Caqar custom. Once regimented under direct control of Peking, the Caqar became available for use in military campaigns both inside and outside China proper ("The Caqar Population during the Ch'ing" [*Journal of Asian History,* XII, 1978, 58-79]).

In the late 18th century, the Ch'ing span of military control reached into the Chinese protectorate of Tibet. John Killigrew describes how the Ch'ien-lung emperor organized an expedition to defend Tibet against the insurgent Gurkha dynasty ("Some Aspects of the Sino-Nepalese War of 1872" [*Journal of Asian History*, XII, 1979, 42-63]). The Gurkhas invaded Tibet in 1788 and 1791. On the first occasion, the Manchu commander sent to deal with the invasion avoided bloodshed by negotiating a settlement favorable to the Gurkhas. But when the Gurkhas made further military moves in 1791, the Ch'ien-lung emperor declared that he had no recourse other than to punish the invaders. Following Confucian conventions which denigrated the use of military force in favor of moral suasion, the emperor wrote that such action "pained his heart" and that all the "people and the officials . . . knew that it was not a great or meritorious deed to be warlike and militaristic." Troops were drawn from the Eight Banners, the force which had led the conquest of China in the 17th century, from the Army of the Green Standard, an exclusively Chinese force, and from military colonies in the border areas. During the long march to Tibet, local officials gave logistics support to the expedition. Once in Tibet, the Ch'ing army quickly captured enemy fortifications on the border and then pursued the Gurkhas into Nepal. The invasion of Nepal taxed Ch'ing supply lines to the limit and the imperial officers and troops were somewhat disoriented by the rapid shift from mountain to jungle fighting. The Ch'ing managed to win only a tactical stand-off at the battle of Nawakot near Katmandu on August 19, 1792. But the Gurkhas were not aware of the exhausted state of the Chinese army and negotiated submission to the Ch'ing.

As essays by Merrilyn Fitzpatrick and Wei Peh T'i indicate, imperial governments did not always rely exclusively on standing armies to achieve military objectives. During the mid-16th century, pirate fleets raided the southeast coast of China. A Ming official named Hu Tsung-hsien was given the task of suppressing the piracy. Fitzpatrick discusses how Hu used his informal connections in the area to augment the official political and military resources at his disposal ("Local Interests and the Anti-Pirate Administration in China's South-east, 1555-1565" [*Ch'ing shih wen-t'i*, IV, 1979, 1-30]). Hu collected a coterie of brilliant literary gentlemen, rather than professional soldiers, to act as his military advisers. These young men also happened to be the scions of wealthy merchant and gentry families willing to contribute funds and prestige to the anti-pirate campaign. This temporary fusion of dynastic and local interests proved effective and the coastal raiders were defeated. Wei describes a similar Ch'ing anti-pirate campaign led by Juan Yuan ("Internal Security and Coastal Control: Juan Yuan and Pirate Suppression in Chekiang, 1799-

1809" [*Ch'ing-shih wen-t'i*, IV, 1979, 83-112]). Juan relied more on official coercion than informal co-optation in his attempt to mobilize local communities to shore up maritime defenses. Juan reactivated the dormant *pao-chia* (mutual guarantee) system of population registration and neighborhood control and used it to raise local militia. He also commissioned a new class of warships based on an Annamese design and purchased foreign-made cannon suitable for naval warfare. Like his Ming predecessor, Juan raised local funds to pay for his military mobilization and modernization schemes.

At the turn of the 18th and 19th centuries, imperial armies faced a new, internal threat in the White Lotus Rebellion (1795-1804), an armed, millenarian movement that was the first in a series of peasant rebellions against Ch'ing rule. The causes of the peasant uprisings may be found in the increasingly unfavorable ratio of people to land, endemic feuding and banditry at the local level, and the persistence, despite government persecution, of devotional religious sects. These uprisings, which reached a peak in scale and intensity in the mid-19th century Taiping Rebellion (1850-1864), exposed what Edward L. Dreyer has termed "catastrophic decay" in the imperial military establishment ("Military Continuities: the PLA and Imperial China," in William Whitson ed., *Military and Political Power in China in the 1970s,* New York, 1972, 3-24). The decay is surprising given the self-conscious warrior mentality and militarism of the Manchus, their success in enlarging the empire and Peking's proven ability to mount spectacular campaigns like the 1791-92 punitive expedition against the Gurkhas. After closer examination, scholars have detected basic flaws in the nature of the Ch'ing military (Richard J. Smith, "Chinese Military Institutions in the Mid-Nineteenth Century, 1850-1860" [*Journal of Asian History*, VII, 1974, 122-161]). Generational change sapped the strength of dynastic military forces because no institutions like military academies developed to train and indoctrinate a professional officer class. Military commanders were typically illiterate and selected only for their ability to wield weapons and lead men in the field. A cultivated Confucian official like Hu Tsung-hsien would not have found the company of such men congenial. Banner and Green Standard troops, numbering 250,000 and 600,000 men respectively, cost two-thirds of the Ch'ing budget. Despite this skewing of revenues toward military purposes, it was well known that the most direct path to public power and private wealth lay through the examination system and the civil bureaucracy. A famous cliche about military service observed that "bad iron is used to make nails and bad men are used to make soldiers."

The "natural" decay of the Ch'ing military was accelerated by the human and financial cost of suppressing the White Lotus Rebellion (Susan Mann Jones and Philip Kuhn, "Dynastic Decline and the Roots of Rebellion," in John K. Fairbank ed., *The Cambridge History*, X, New York, 1978). During the rebellion, Ch'ing officials discovered that the White Lotus Sect could only be crushed by mobilizing the support of local elites. The same kind of fusion of dynastic and local interests which had frustrated the designs of pirate fleets, worked to frustrate the millenarian dreams of peasant rebels. But the need to resort to this kind of military improvisation—gentry led and financed local armies—signified, according to Jones and Kuhn, the "irreversible decline of Ch'ing military power."

Less than 40 years after the suppression of the White Lotus Rebellion, the Ch'ing military was decisively beaten by the British in the Opium War (1839-1842). A decade after that defeat the dynasty was nearly overthrown by Taiping rebels. The British victory can be explained by the West's superior military technology (iron steamships, field artillery and flintlock muskets) and the limited objectives of the imperialist powers (Frederick Wakeman, "The Canton Trade and the Opium War," in Fairbank, 1978). The near success and final defeat of the Taiping movement were due to a complex of strategic, political and social factors.

Battles are important, as Frederick Engles' paraphrase of Clausewitz suggests: "Fighting is to war what cash payment is to trade, for however rarely it may be necessary for it to actually occur, everything is directed towards it, and eventually it must take place all the same and must be decisive" (quoted by John Keegan, *The Face of Battle*, New York, 1976, p. 30). In late imperial China, "everything directed towards" fighting included the emergence of rebel armies from devotional religious sects. Hung Hsiu-ch'uan was the founder of the Taiping movement (T'ai-p'ing t'ien-Kuo, "Heavenly Kingdom of Great Peace") and believed himself to be the younger brother of Jesus Christ. In a context of ethnic feuds (Hung and many of his followers belonged to the Hakka ethnic minority) and persecution by the Ch'ing government, Hung's "Society of God Worshippers" took up arms against the state and the Confucian establishment. When a Ch'ing army attempted to suppress the movement in the southern province of Kwangsi where it had originated, the rebels broke out of the encirclement and marched north to the Yangtze River. There, in 1852, they captured the important walled city of Wuch'ang. At this point, the Taiping leaders faced a critical choice in terms of strategy. With imperial armies in retreat, should the rebels continue their drive north toward Peking or should they consolidate their position in Central China? After heated debate, the rebels decided on the latter course. They sailed downstream, captured Nanking and established a rival Taiping dynasty. Many scholars believe that had the rebel armies marched north after the fall of Wuch'ang, they would have succeeded in toppling the Ch'ing government. In his essay, "Strategical Problems of the Taipings in the Early Years of their Rebellion," People's Republic of China (PRC) historian Chang Yi-wen disagrees (*Li-shih yen-chiu*, 1979, 20–30). Chang believes the decision to postpone a northern expedition made sense from both military and political points of view. He argues that logistics and supply problems involved in a precipitous march across the North China plain would have doomed the enterprise. Moreover, Chang insists that the Taiping rebels needed time to apply and consolidate their revolutionary program of land redistribution. Echoing Clausewitz and every Chinese military thinker from Sun Wu to Mao Tse-tung, Chang argues that "military affairs must yield to politics."

The decision to try to rule from Nanking gave Ch'ing forces time and opportunity to lay siege to the city from camps north and south of the Yangtze. Siegecraft, uncomplicated by modern artillery, was one of the few strengths of the mid-19th century Ch'ing standing armies. Chang Yi-wen believes that if the Taiping army had attacked the Ch'ing camps in force and then committed all their resources to an attack north to Peking, the Taiping movement might still have succeeded. Instead the rebels broke up their forces into several armies, sending only one column north. That expedition was destroyed by Ch'ing forces near Tientsin in 1855.

Chang also attributes the failure of the Taiping movement to its religious or "superstitious" aspects. Chang's ambivalence toward the conscious goals of an archaic rural uprising has recently been carried further in a major reinterpretation of "peasant wars" like the White Lotus and Taiping rebellions. In the past, historians of the PRC tended to regard peasant wars as the highest and purest expression of class conflict. Each peasant rebellion was supposed to have left the peasantry freer of feudal ties and obligations. Now Jung Sheng and others claim this glorification of peasant wars was the result of doctrinaire thinking and the pernicious influence of Lin Piao and the "Gang of Four" ("Have Peasant Wars Constituted the Only Real Motive Force in the Historical Development of China's Feudal Society?" [*Li-shih yen-chiu*, 1979, 49–56]). Jung Sheng urges a more skeptical accounting of the causes and consequences of peasant wars. In effect, he is asking historians to release the idea of class warfare from the strictures of historical inevitability and make the conduct and outcome of peasant wars as problematical as conflicts decided on battlefields tend to be. Many peasant wars were bloody disasters which simply served to tighten controls over the peasantry by building up the military capability of local elites.

In fact the initial success of the Taiping peasant war set in motion a chain of events which greatly strengthened the military power of the monied and propertied classes in the countryside. Banner and Green Standard troops could not defeat the rebels. Instead the task of repression was handled by what Richard J. Smith terms "temporary or non-regular" armies. The Taiping threat required a massive intervention by local elites in military affairs. Following the pioneering work of Philip Kuhn (*Rebellion and Its Enemies in Late Imperial China,* Cambridge, Mass., 1970), Smith describes how new regional and local armies were personally raised by gentry members in and out of the government who were appalled by the revolutionary, anti-Confucian program of the Taipings. Chang Yi-wen describes approvingly in his essay how the Taiping leaders postponed a decisive thrust north in 1852 in order to consolidate their revolution. However, this hesitation, and active display of the Taiping's revolutionary intent, provided the impetus for an improvised countermobilization by supporters of the status quo.

In military crises, the imperial government was accustomed to delegating vast military powers to civil officials, even arming and mobilizing the populace if necessary. This loan of military power was supposed to be temporary and to be retrieved after the crisis had past. Civilian officials, conscious of careers which wove in and out of civil and military assignments, had no reason to oppose this demobilization. But the removal of weapons and military expertise placed in the hands of local elites and their followers proved to be a thornier problem. Periodic militarization of society, often at least initially sanctioned by the government, led to a residue of violence in the areas affected. Harry Lamley describes how weapons and militia first used for community defense could subsequently contribute to endemic violence in the resolution of private disputes and feuds (*"Hsieh-tou:* The Pathology of Violence in Southeastern China" [*Ch'ing-shih wen-t'i*, III, 1977, 1–39]). Lamley believes that these habits of violence contributed to the emergence of 19th-century rebellions like the Taiping movement.

Aside from this defect, military improvisations which made civil officials temporarily into "militarists" and created elite-directed communities-in-arms provided a cost effective way of responding to local military crises. But during the Taiping Rebellion this devolution of authority was so extensive as to defy post-war attempts to demobilize society and retrieve military power from control of local elites. In some frontier areas the Ch'ing government was forced to tolerate the presence of entire outlaw armies created during the Taiping disorders (Ella S. Laffey, "Social Dissidence and Government Suppression on the Sino-Vietnamese Frontier: The

Black Flag Army in Tonkin'' [*Ch'ing-shih wen-t'i*, IV, 1979, 113-125]). Throughout rural China local landlord and gentry classes used fortified villages, weapons and militia, and the taxing power to support these military instruments, to increase their power at the expense of the peasantry and the Ch'ing government.

This shift in military power downward contrasts with the experience of other premodern regimes. As Perry Anderson has written in his study of European absolutism, the end of feudalism witnessed a "displacement of politico-legal coercion upwards toward a centralized, militarized summit—the Absolutist state" (*The Absolutist State in the West*, London, 1974, p. 19). In the 19th century the Ch'ing state, confronted by massive peasant rebellion and intractable foreign threats, did not become a "centralized, militarized summit." The "unprofessional" nature of its civilian-dominated military institutions made such a transformation difficult to countenance or effect. The conventional Marxist periodization of Chang Yi-wen and Jung Sheng notwithstanding, China did not have a feudal, militarized landowning class which could be forced, or convinced, to relinquish its powers to a centralized state. Facing a financial crisis brought on by the huge expense of fielding professional armies, absolutist states, and their constitutional successors, borrowed the centrally located wealth of emerging capitalist economies. Chinese society, with its commercially developed, but preindustrial economy, could not offer comparable support for a centralized, professional military establishment.

However, a long string of defeats in military competition with imperialist powers finally compelled the Ch'ing, in its last decades, to move in the direction of military modernization. The ability of even relatively weak modern armies to suppress peasant rebellion provided added incentive for change. The premier example of institutional support for a more militarized state was the creation of the New Armies after 1900. The Ch'ing regime used these foreign trained and equipped forces to protect the capital and garrison strategic cities in the provinces. Unfortunately for the Ch'ing, the expense and complexities of building a modern army created conditions ripe for mutiny against the throne and for an alliance between opposition politicians and modern, professional soldiers.

In his essay, "Elite Militarism, Popular Tax Protest and China's National Revolution," John Fincher describes how military reforms and the required budgets became contributing factors in the overthrow of the Ch'ing (*Papers on Far Eastern History*, March 1979, 223-236). In 1910 and 1911, in the context of Russian and Japanese military threats in North China, the Court and Ministries in Peking, provincial officials and the new gentry-dominated provincial assemblies quarreled among themselves in a restrained way about the size of provincial contributions to the support of the New Armies. In some provinces over half the provincial budget went to pay for the new forces and taxes levied for this purpose triggered periodic and violent protests.

Provincial politicians questioned the size of military budgets and the consequences for local society. The unspoken issue was who would control this expensive, new military organization. In February 1911 Chinese students in Japan raised this latter, highly controversial issue. Japanese universities, colleges and military academies provided trained personnel for Ch'ing reform projects like the New Armies. Concerned about recent Russian and Japanese military threats, Chinese students in Tokyo staged protests and published propaganda materials calling for the mobilization of a vast, popular army.

The Ch'ing regime did all it could to suppress this idea, but it surfaced in altered form among dissident provincial politicians who gathered in Peking in the spring of 1911 to debate what kind of army China should have. They considered various types of traditional militia organizations and then decided to promote a system of reserve forces, presumably more responsive than the New Armies to provincial interests. Fincher believes that, at the same time, gentry politicians were discussing ways to modernize and consolidate their post-Taiping local military power, the radical ideas of Chinese students in Japan were penetrating the New Army through the return of cadet graduates to their units. This migration of radical ideas explains the documented rise of nationalistic and revolutionary feeling among New Army soldiers in 1911.

Fincher also speculates that military cadets trained in Japan may have consciously or unconsciously adopted the Japanese idea of an activist role in politics for soldiers. As a result, in October 1911 New Army units became predisposed to side not with the Ch'ing regime but with the revolutionaries. Modern armies are expensive and the new taxes they require can expose military policy to scrutiny by the people who pay them. Modern armies also require highly trained men and sophisticated materiel. In this case, young cadets brought back from Japan both military expertise and also politically subversive nationalistic and revolutionary sentiments and, if Fincher is correct, the un-Confucian idea that soldiers need not remain subordinate to civilians.

In late imperial China, large standing armies existed. But the prevailing bias for civil administration and against military institutions, in combination with the regime's tolerance of "temporary armies," inhibited the militarization of the state. However, in a context of peasant rebellion and foreign imperialism, state resistance to militarism contributed to a militarization of society.

The development of the New Armies constituted a major exception to this decentralization of military power. As described by Edmund S. K. Fung, the New Army forces reached a peak in efficiency and fighting spirit just prior to the 1911 Revolution ("Revolution and the Chinese Army, 1911-1913" [*Papers on Far Eastern History*, 1979, 13-54]). New Army units were so much more effective than revolutionary armies raised from scratch in 1911, that the mutiny and defection of New Army troops proved the decisive factor in the overthrow of the Ch'ing. The New Armies then turned against their revolutionary allies and supported the presidency of New Army commander Yuan Shih-kai.

The New Army in 1911 and 1912 represented a singular moment in Chinese military history, when a modern, professional force successfully emerged from the ambiguous late imperial legacy of degenerate Banner and Green Standard troops and uncontrollable local militia. But, as Fung suggests, the New Army was ultimately "disorganized by the Revolution." Discipline was relaxed, a less stringent recruitment policy damaged the corporate integrity of the regiments, and officers became affiliated with various political factions. In the aftermath of the 1911 Revolution the tentative connection between centralized state power and a modern military establishment was broken.

Warlordism was the result of this broken connection. For a time, as Andrew Nathan has shown, military power was expressed as or even off-set by bureaucratic and parliamentary intrigues in Peking (*Peking Politics 1918-1923: Factionalism and the Failure of Constitutionalism*, Berkeley, 1976). By the mid-1920s, regionally based militarists still campaigned to seize control of Peking and the legitimacy that possession of the city could confer. But they were in no respect dependent on a central government for resources or recognition.

One obvious approach to the study of an era of warring militarists is biographical. Biographers of warlords typically contrast their protagonist with the conventional notion that militarists were little more than gangsters. Not surprisingly, these scholars have discovered some positive feature of each militarist's rule—a progressive idea or project—which undermines the stereotype of the warlord as an amoral brute. Kuangtung militarist Ch'en Chiung-ming wanted to modernize his home province (Winston Hsieh, "The Ideas and Ideals of a Warlord: Ch'en Chiung-ming (1878-1933)" [*Harvard Papers on China*, XVI, 1962, 198-252]). Yen

Hsi-shan attempted to reconstruct and reform local government (Donald G. Gillin, *Warlord: Yen Hsi-shan in Shansi Province, 1911-1949,* Princeton, 1967). Feng Yu-hsiang meticulously cared for his troops and experimented with ideas and policies culled from Christianity and Marxism (James E. Sheridan, *Chinese Warlord: The Career of Feng Yu-hsiang,* Stanford, 1966). Culturally polished Wu P'ei-fu, who had passed the Ch'ing civil service examinations as a youth, was regarded by some as a "Confucian" warlord (Odoric Y. K. Wou, *Militarism in Modern China: The Career of Wu P'ei-fu,* Canberra, 1978). The "good official" who blended or alternated civilian and military leadership roles remained a powerful image in the Republican period even though the institutional and moral supports for dual careers as scholar-official and military strategist had disappeared. While warlords based their power on the day to day command of armies, for practical and ideological reasons they invariably attempted to govern, as well as garrison, their territories.

In fact, some scholars have argued that territory explains more about the behavior of militarists than degree of deviation from a modal warlord personality. Chang Tso-lin's base in strategically important and resource rich Manchuria made periodic intervention in North China irresistible (Gavin McCormack, *Chang Tso-lin in Northeast China, 1911-1928: China, Japan and the Manchurian Idea,* Stanford, 1977). Access to revenue from the lucrative opium traffic made Yunnan warlords financially secure and indifferent to outside threats and opportunities (John C. S. Hall, *The Yunnan Provincial Faction, 1927-1937,* Canberra, 1976). Provincialism lent the "Kwangsi Clique" a cohesive political posture which served these militarists well in struggles for power at the national level (Diana Lary, *Region and Nation: The Kwangsi Clique in Chinese Politics, 1925-1937,* Cambridge, 1974).

Competition among individual militarists, as they sought to preserve or expand their territories, persisted long enough to produce a "system of military separatism" (C. Martin Wilbur, "Military Separatism and the Process of Reunification under the Nationalist Regime, 1922-1937," in Ping-ti Ho and Tang Tsou eds., *China in Crisis,* vol. I, Chicago, 1968, 203-263). This system imposed itself on militarists and anti-militarists alike. By the 1920s, to qualify as a serious political contender on the national, or even local level, individuals like the militarists listed above and political groupings like the Kuomintang (KMT) or the Chinese Communist Party (CCP) all needed the control of an army.

Each contender attempted to carve out a territory based on intentions which imperfectly balanced ambitions and capabilities (Harold Z. Schiffrin, "Military and Politics in China: Is the Warlord Model Pertinent?" [*Asia Quarterly*, III, 1975, 193-206]). Chi Hsi-sheng argues that militarism as a system was analogous to a constellation of competing nation states. The resulting balance of power was upset whenever a particular contender acquired a new military capability (*Warlord Politics in China, 1916-1928*, Stanford, 1976). Winston Hsieh suggests that the system was also unstable because administrative units controlled by warlords rarely exactly coincided with regional economic systems ("The Economics of Warlordism" [*Chinese Republican Studies Newsletter*, I, 1975, 15-21]). There was always some coveted economic resource just over the border and the search by armies for these scarce resources often triggered military conflict or channeled campaigns.

Jerome Ch'en claims that military control of civil administration and extraction of economic resources had extraordinary and negative effects on Chinese society and the economy (*The Military-Gentry Coalition: China Under the Warlords*, University of Toronto-York University Joint Centre on Modern East Asia, Publication Series, vol. I, 1978). Mid-19th century rebellions and their suppression militarized China's gentry class. Gentry members, in the process, forged alliances with military men and used their expertise to defend and then enlarge local elite power. According to Ch'en, this coalition continued intact throughout the first half of the 20th century. But the rise of regional militarism placed military men, not the gentry, in the dominant position. Military-gentry regimes at all levels of society siphoned off much of China's available resources for use in wasteful factional struggles and to maintain large standing armies. Ch'en argues that, during the long era from mid-19th century rebellion to mid-20th century Communist victory, militarism and militarization severely retarded China's modernization.

Other research suggests a more ambiguous economic legacy for militarism. Ronald Suleski describes the success achieved by Chang Tso-lin's Manchurian regime in currency reform ("The Rise and Fall of the Fengtien Dollar, 1917-1928: Currency Reform in Warlord China" [*Modern Asian Studies* XIII, 1979, 643-660]). Following Jerome Ch'en's line of reasoning, warlord regimes are usually pictured as incapable of reform. The fact that creation of a stable currency made tax collection easier and facilitated domestic and foreign trade may explain the concurrence of wills and interests in support of the measure. Suleski also describes how Chang Tso-lin wrecked the currency reform during his final military campaigns on the North China plain. Chang simply printed money to finance the cost of military competition.

From the perspective of a city or community under siege, warlord armies appeared enormous and momentarily decisive. But on a macro-societal level, as Thomas Rawski has recently pointed out, these same armies appear small, starved for resources and bound to China's limited railway and highway network (*China's Republican Economy: An Introduction,* University of Toronto-York University Joint Centre on Modern East Asia, Publication Series, vol. I, 1978). Rawski criticizes historians who assume, like Jerome Ch'en, that militarism dominated or substantially obstructed the economy. Using available statistics on the size and scope of operations of regional armies, Rawski shows that, measured against the vast Chinese population, the effects of militarism were rather limited. Military spending consumed three to four per cent of the GNP. Only 2 per cent of males between the ages of 15 and 44 served in the military. War dead, both civilian and military, account for one percent of total mortality. Many provincial or "national" armies consumed half to two-thirds of government budgets. But these budgets were themselves tiny. Militarism periodically victimized particular communities and may have undermined long term investment. But armies themselves, and the troops who served in them, suffered from the weak fiscal position of the governments they seized or were allied with. Although armies were often strong enough to militarize the summits of civil administration, possession of the machinery of government did not give soldiers much leverage in transforming or even controlling society.

Throughout the Republican period, no single state power came close to monopolizing the means of organized violence. The Peking government in the early teens, Chiang Kai-shek's Nanking regime in the mid-1930s and Japanese occupation forces in the early forties all exerted military and political control over large areas of China. But each faced one or more rival governments. Under these conditions public and private armies proliferated. Nor was military competition restricted to the national and regional levels. Rival regimes could extend their span of control over provincial and regional lines, yet they could not garrison and defend most small towns and villages. In this power vacuum, or sometimes in direct continuity with post-Taiping militarization of local society, a myriad of small and large armed bands sprang up and competed for power and resources. Many operated openly as bandits; others had some claim to formal governmental authority.

Reflecting on the endemic nature of violence in this period, Guy Alitto argues that regional militarism and local militarization both expressed a "cultural crisis" ("Rural Elites in Transition: China's Cultural Crisis and the Problem of Legitimacy,'' in Susan Mann Jones ed., *Select Papers from the Center for Far Eastern Studies,* University of Chicago, vol. III, 1978–79, 218–275). The Republican symbol of ''the people'' had failed to provide an effective substitute for the legitimating roles of Confucian values and the emperor. At all levels, almost without exception, organized violence corrupted civil institutions. Since no common moral code or allegiance had any claim on political leaders, they all behaved like bandits. The rule of violence applied to ''government armies, private armies, bandit organizations and, to a degree, party armies.''

By the mid-1930s, within the limits imposed by fiscal weakness and a partially modernized communications system, the Nationalists had won a position of military dominance over domestic rivals. The KMT had forced the Communists to flee the cities and to take refuge in the impoverished border regions between provinces. The Nationalists were strong enough to win battlefield victories over domestic rivals but not strong enough to resist the Japanese. In 1937, in a series of lightning campaigns, Japanese armies drove the KMT from the eastern half of China to sanctuary behind the easily defensible gorges which mark the eastern approach to Szechuan Province.

During wartime, a new Communist-led military force emerged which was capable of winning battles, if not the war, against the KMT and the Japanese. Because of earlier military defeats, the Communists inhabited the same territory bandits thrived in—the peripheral border regions. City-based armies, though superior in military organization and firepower, found it difficult to approach and control areas not accessible by modern transportation. In the early thirties, only an extraordinary KMT effort, aided by German military advisors, had pried the Communists from their Kiangsi redoubt and forced them to retreat on the Long March to Yenan. Ironically, military defeat gave the Communists the opportunity to build a new army from the bottom up.

One measure of the Communists' new, and ultimately successful, approach to military affairs was their policy toward bandits. In both imperial and early Republican periods, government armies absorbed bandit units by co-opting their leaders. In his essay ''The Wartime Communists and their Local Rivals: Bandits and Secret Societies,'' Ch'en Yung-fa analyses the CCP's radically different strategy (*Select Papers from the Center for Far Eastern Studies,* vol. III, 1978–79, 1–69). Bandit or ex-bandit units tended to form a ragged edge, too expensive to mend, of town or city-based armies.

The Communists were based in peripheral areas and dependent on the vitality of small, popularly supported guerrilla forces. They therefore could not tolerate undisciplined troops, given to banditry and feuding, so close to the center of their power. As Alitto suggests, any political force operating in this environment risked becoming like bandits. Since the Communists needed all the manpower they could get, they accepted the bandit units into the Red Army, but only after they had been broken up and deprived of their original leaders. Indoctrination and the fostering of new bases of group solidarity made armies recruited in militarized and bandit-ridden border regions responsive to Communist commands.

After the Japanese invasion in 1937, Communist forces grew rapidly. Twenty years ago, Chalmers Johnson offered his "peasant nationalism" hypothesis to explain the CCP's wartime success. He argued that the shock of the Japanese invasion created a new peasant consciousness of nationhood and made the peasantry available for mobilization by the Communists (*Peasant Nationalism and Communist Power: The Emergence of Revolutionary China 1937-49*, Stanford, 1962). Critics have charged that Johnson wrongly ignored the importance of the CCP's social appeal to tenant farmers and other aggrieved rural inhabitants (Donald G. Gillin, " 'Peasant Nationalism' and the History of Chinese Communism" [*Journal of Asian Studies*, XXIII, 1964, 269-289]). In a recent article, Johnson defends his original argument without apology ("Peasant Nationalism Revisited: The Biography of a Book" [*China Quarterly*, LXXII, 1977, 766-785]). He states that anyone who cannot see the decisive importance of World War II as it affected China, does not understand the social consequences of large-scale armed conflict.

Johnson draws an image of Japanese armies cutting swaths of destruction and terror across China, dramatically altering the condition and consciousness of those in their paths. The Japanese armies were easily more powerful and destructive than any previous military force operating in China. Like their warlord and Nationalist predecessors, however, Japanese armies hugged the railways and all-weather roads. The impact of the invasion could not be uniform and it is unlikely that the Japanese presence produced a uniformly nationalistic peasantry.

One way in which the mobilization effect favored by Johnson might be made more specific and precise is through the use of the idea of "spontaneous mobilization" developed by Kataoka Tetsuya and discussed by Ch'en Yung-fa in his article (*Resistance and Revolution in China: The Communists and the Second United Front*, Berkeley, 1974). The weeks, or perhaps months, following the Japanese rout of the KMT did indeed create a rural panic and a power vacuum. Peasants were willing to follow anyone with a scintilla of skill in military and political affairs. In some areas the

Communists were able to capitalize on the disorganizing effect of war on the countryside. Nevertheless, they too were often thrown into disarray. By the time the CCP had reordered its forces, calm had returned to communities and peasants and local elites had begun to make peace with the Japanese occupation forces. To reinsert themselves as a military and political force the Communists used their well-honed organizational skills and the considerable room for maneuver left by the urban-based Japanese occupation.

During the wartime and civil war periods, the present-day outlines of the People's Liberation Army (PLA) became visible. The contemporary PLA is in many respects an unusual military force. It is "multifunctional": it does other things besides fighting or preparing to fight. For example, soldiers grow some of their own food; they supply nightsoil to peasants; they manage major sectors of Chinese industry; the officer corps participates extensively in politics at the highest level. But despite, or perhaps because of, its immense power the military has never carried out a coup (with the possible exception of Lin Piao's alleged attempt to assassinate Mao). The distinction between civilian and military realms is often blurred, and yet it is possible to discern a definite professional current throughout the PLA's history.

As Edward Dreyer has pointed out, some features of the contemporary PLA suggest continuities with the imperial past. Early in his career as a Communist and a soldier, Mao warned against a "purely military viewpoint" and insisted that "the Party must command the gun." This squares with traditional ideological and institutional controls on military power. The Ch'ing regime tolerated local militia; the PRC also maintains a part-time soldiery—although, as the Gang of Four's unsuccessful attempt to subvert the urban militia indicates, the army strives to keep these organizations under tight control (Alan P. Liu, "The 'Gang of Four' and the Chinese People's Liberation Army" [*Asian Survey*, XX, 1979, 817–837]). One important difference between imperial times and the contemporary military, and an example of continuity with the early 20th century, is the importance now attached to soldiering as a professional career. Soldiers are no longer thought of as "bad iron" or rough mannered warriors.

Many of the unique qualities of the Chinese officer corps, as Jonathan Adelman suggests, have their origin in the wartime and civil war periods ("Origins of the Difference in Political Influence of the Soviet and Chinese Armies: The Officer Corps in the Civil Wars" [*Studies in Comparative Communism*, X, 1977, 347–369]). The Russian Communists fought their civil war with a hastily assembled collection of ex-Tsarist officers, partisan fighters and newly minted Soviet officers. The Soviets evolved an elaborate system of Party and secret police controls to guarantee the loyalty of this politically suspect and fractious class of military leaders. This traumatic period in the history of the Red Army bequeathed a fear of Bonapartism to civilian leaders and a strictly limited role in politics for the military. In contrast, as a result of its early military defeats and exile to the hinterland, the Chinese Red Army had years to train and indoctrinate its officer corps before its decisive battles with the Nationalists. Because of early high attrition of officers from the CCP's urban years, officers recruited in the 1930s and 1940s numerically dominated the corps of military leaders. Most of these men had similar, rural backgrounds. Because of the need to maintain constant military vigilance, a virtual fusion between party and army took place, reducing the need for elaborate checks on the latter. As a new, citizen army leading a popular insurrection, the PLA, unlike the early Soviet army, quickly became a model for the new revolutionary society.

After 1949, the Communists established a strong connection between centralized state.and modern army. With the exception of the brief New Army interlude at the turn of the century, this connection was unprecedented in Chinese history. Also unprecedented is the present link between the military and a modern industrial sector: as Harlan Jencks points out in a major new work on the PLA, the Chinese army has access to a large and growing military-industrial complex (*From Muskets to Missiles: Politics and Professionalism in the Chinese Army, 1945–1980,* forthcoming). The links are likely to be decisive in promoting military professionalism, defined by Jencks as a commitment to "specialization, efficiency and national security." The close of more than a century of rebellion, revolution and civil war occurred when the PRC achieved a virtual monopoly over the means of violence in society. The Chinese populace was disarmed and the state fostered a separation of military and politico-administrative functions and began to buy and produce sophisticated military hardware. These forces promise to confine future Chinese military history to bureaucratic politics and border wars.

David Strand is on the faculty of Dickinson College. Ming K. Chan is on the faculty of U.C.L.A. and is a research fellow at the Hoover Institution.

Journals Consulted

Asia Quarterly • Asian Survey • China Quarterly • Chinese Republican Studies Newsletter • Ch'ing-shih wen-t'i • Journal of Asian History • Jour-

nal of Asian Studies • *Li-shih yen-chiu* • *Modern Asian Studies* • *Papers on Far Eastern History* (Australian National University) • *Select Papers from the Center for Far Eastern Studies* (University of Chicago) • *Studies in Comparative Communism.*

THE UNITED STATES: WOMEN IN WORLD WAR II

Rebecca S. Greene

Central to the discussion of World War II in recent years has been the extent to which the war changed American society. Richard S. Kirkendall in *The United States: 1929–1945* (New York, 1974) expresses the opinion of one group of historians that despite the crisis of World War II little happened to change American social, political, and economic institutions. In sharp contrast, Richard Polenberg in *War and Society* (New York, 1972) contends that a major transformation occurred. That such a transformation affected the status of women is most cogently argued in William Chafe's *The American Woman* (New York, 1972). While many recent historians would agree with Chafe that a major transformation occurred during the war, some would argue this change was only temporary.

One way to evaluate the degree of change is to examine the labor force. In "Women Workers in World War II: Michigan as a Test Case" (*Labor History*, XX, 1979, 44–72) Alan Clive notes that women in the labor force jumped from 10.8 million in March 1941 to over 18 million by August 1944. In Michigan the rise was even greater, more than doubling from 391,600 in March 1940 to 799,100 by November 1943, the peak of the war. Women entered industry in record numbers especially in previously male fields. According to Nancy Gabin in "Women Workers and the UAW in the Post-World War II Period" (*Labor History*, XXI, 1979, 5–30) "in 1939, there were an estimated 3,130 female production workers in the transportation equipment and automobile industries; in November 1943 there were 77,400 . . . an increase of nearly 2,500 per cent."

But perhaps the greatest difference was in the composition of the female labor force. Before the war, according to Chafe and Clive, working women were young, single, and poor. From World War II on, a majority were married, at least 35 years old, and middle class. Employers who before the war had been reluctant to hire middle-aged or married women now welcomed them. Encouraging such a change was a broadening in the rationale for women working. In contrast to the Depression, where most women worked to forestall poverty, starting in World War II women worked not only out of economic necessity but to sustain or improve their middle-class standard of living, for example, to pay for the education of children or the purchase of a home. In addition, for the first time in American history the national government supported day-care centers, giving women with pre-school children the option to work.

According to Clive, Michigan manufacturers refused to hire more than 2,000 women out of a War Manpower Commission call for 40,000. They also evaded state equal pay regulations and discriminated against black female workers by placing them in menial jobs. In "Working Women and World War II" (*New England Quarterly,* 1980, 42–61) Marc Miller finds that women in Lowell, Massachusetts moved from their traditional work in textile mills to more remunerative work in wartime industry, only to find it more tedious and subject to the same lack of equal pay. Looking at how policy decisions were made about women during the War, Eleanor Straub in "U.S. Government Policy Toward Civilian Women" (*Prologue,* V, 1973, 240–254) notes that female labor conscription got nowhere despite widespread popular support. Day-care was inadequate, and recommendations for special health and safety standards for women were largely ignored because federal agencies gave women little role in decision making. Put in minor advisory committees, their primary function during the war was not to enforce but to publicize the government's program for working women. Straub attributes the lack of influence of female policy makers to two factors: the prejudice of men who assumed all women to be "housewives"; and the organizational problems of these women, who diffused their energies in too many directions and failed to get outside support. An even grimmer assessment of "change" appears in "Women in the War Economy—World War II" (*Review of Radical Political Economics,* IV, 1972, 40–57), where Joan Trey maintains that the social attitudes of men and women towards women working were scarcely altered. According to Trey, men continued to believe that women did not deserve equal pay since they did not have to support a family, and were less capable, more frequently absent, and slow to fight for their rights. That family responsibilities might impinge on the union participation of women or that unions did little for women was not considered. Although the thinking of women may have been more progressive than men, they suffered in their fight for advancement by being new to the field, with little knowledge of their rights and low union membership.

The resistance against women working was especially apparent where women competed with men in previously all-male fields. In "Women in the Shipyard" (*Radical America*, IX, 1975, 139–145) Katherine Archibald, a trained sociologist who spent two years during the war as store keeper and clerk in shipyards, recalls that men frequently gossiped about the promiscuity of certain women and the mechanical ineptitude and laziness of others. As a result of such stories, management imposed strict rules on the attire of female welders and construction workers, while allowing women in the more traditional secretary and bookkeeping fields to wear whatever they pleased. Similarly, in the industrial town of Lowell, where women also took on male jobs, Miller finds that fear of sexual fraternization led employers to enforce rigid, sometimes unpleasant rules about conduct between women and men. Not only male attitudes placed stress on women, as Augusta Clauson illustrates in "Shipyard Diary of a Woman Welder" (*Radical America*, IX, 1975, 134–138). Clauson recalls her earliest experiences as a shipwelder, climbing stairs despite her fear of heights, fearful of falling because she had little experience with such situations. Nor was it easy for her co-worker, one of whose seven children had just been drafted, to go on welding as if nothing had happened.

Despite these limitations, one should not conclude that there was scarcely any change in the socio-economic role of the American woman. The point is not that there was some resistance or that the opportunities for women paled before an absolute standard, but that the degree of participation of women in World War II showed a decided increase from previous decades. One way to measure how World War II differed from the past is to look at another 20th-century military crisis, World War I. Two excellent articles on labor in World War I are: Maureen Weiner Greenwald, "Women Workers and World War I: The American Railroad Industry, a Case Study" (*Journal of Social History*, IX, 1975, 154–177), and Valerie J. Conner, " 'The Mothers of the Race' in World War I: The National War Labor Board and Women in Industry" (*Labor History*, XXI, 1979–80, 33–54). These indicate that the First World War offered fewer opportunities for women and reflected more conservative attitudes towards women working.

Statistically, 1.5 million women worked in World War I compared to as many as 18 million in World War II. Women in World War I were employed as streetcar and railroad conductors, welders, electricians, truckers, and blacksmiths, but their representation in such traditionally male fields was much smaller than during World War II. According to Greenwald, women in the railroad industry occupied only a few hundred traditionally male slots, while women telegraph operators accounted for no more than 2.4 per cent of the field. This declined to 1 per cent shortly after the war.

Unlike World War II, in World War I most female job holders had worked before and were generally restricted to the young, the single, and the working class; in the railroad industry, only a fifth of the women were newcomers. Most of these women were either widows, spouses deserted by soldier husbands, or fiancees waiting for their men to return home, and usually they worked only for the duration of the war. Attitudes against women working were more blatantly exhibited in the First World War than in the Second. Ironically, it was the concern of the Progressive Era about the health of the potential mother which became the paramount rationale for restricting the number of women in "strenuous" male jobs during the war and dismissing them afterwards, although a second argument, more prominent in World War I than later, was the Victorian notion that the woman need not work since her husband could support her.

Even if one were to accept the notion of wartime "transformation" in the status of women, however, some historians argue that whatever change occurred was shortlived. In Lowell, Miller notes, a quarter of women in factories lost their jobs during three months of 1946. In Detroit, according to Clive, women in industry declined from 124,000 in March 1945 to 66,000 by the close of the year, only 20,000 more than in 1940. Results nationwide were no better: the number of women in the work force was down to 29 per cent in August, 1946, from a high during the War of 36 per cent.

Contributing to this decline was a social pressure to return home. In "Prescription for Penelope: Literature on Women's Obligations to the Returning World War II Veterans" (*Women's Studies*, V, 1978, 223-229) Susan M. Hartmann notes that government, psychiatric, sociological, and popular literature all stressed that the woman must accommodate herself to the returning veteran because he would need her sympathy and flexibility in readjusting to civilian life. Besides stressing that the woman must tolerate closeness with former buddies or even extramarital affairs (something not condoned for women), the literature particularly emphasized that a woman must give up both her wartime attitudes of independence (generated by years of separation) and her job. Employers took a more direct approach. As Clive notes, not only were women "last hired the first fired" in the recession immediately following the war, but in Michigan factories transferred women to heavy lifting jobs, in some cases illegally, and put all women on the midnight shift. Unions did not interfere; Walter Reuther of the UAW informed the Women's Conference in 1944 that "women could expect no special privileges to enable them to hold on to their jobs."

Whatever social tolerance toward women working existed during the emergency of war seemed to subside afterwards.

Yet Chafe would still argue that the change in the role of women and the attitudes of society towards women working continued after the war. While admitting a drop in female employment from 1945–1947, he nevertheless notes that by 1949 women were returning to the labor force, bringing the number way above the level of 1940. And even female industrial labor, which had shown a decline of over one million in 1946, still included more women in late 1946 than in 1940. Moreover, it continued to be socially acceptable for middle-class, middle-aged wives to work to raise the family standard of living.

Although Chafe is correct that the number of women employed after the war continued to be above the level of 1940, he ignores the fact that there was a particular growth in clerical and sales work, the kind of work which was less remunerative and more unskilled. There was a continued decline in the number of professional women (as Chafe himself says), and according to Ruth Meyerowitz in ''Women Unionists and World War II'' (unpublished paper, Organization of American Historians, New York, 1980) a switching of female industrial labor from high-skill to low-skill work. Although the trend for married women to work continued in the postwar period, a close look at the figures indicates that they probably were mothers with older children, not preschoolers as often occurred during the war. This conclusion can also be supported by Chafe's own evidence: he notes the ''median age of workers (between 1940 and 1950) rose from 32 to 36 and a half'' and the ''number of women workers aged 18 to 24 declined 8 per cent and those from 35 to 54 gained 77 per cent.'' Thus the group most likely to be going to the suburbs with young children declined in the employment figures.

A review of the periodical literature shows that historians disagree on the extent of change in the status of women during and after the war. They also disagree on the reasons for change, or the lack of it. Those who argue that little alteration in the role of women occurred come to similar conclusions about causation, and attribute the lack of change to the internalization of the conventional female role. To support this contention, they point to the fact that women were loath to use day-care and willingly gave up work for family after the war. This group of historians maintains that American women neither took advantage of institutions to liberate themselves nor resisted pressures on them to withdraw from the labor force.

There are problems with this interpretation, however. For one thing,

Clive argues that women did not use day-care because they preferred care by relatives or friends. Without going through the internal records of agencies, we know little about the condition of day-care, such as the quality of facilities or the training of staff. What we do know suggests that underuse (as low as 10 per cent of capacity) was caused by the unsuitability of available services. As Chafe notes, government grants for day-care rarely went above the minimal sum of $7,000; the Lanham Act provided for no more than half the funding, with the rest to come from the local community. Clive notes that the local, state, and federal bureaucracies stalled funds for the establishment of centers. Use was also discouraged by the reluctance of government and employer to place centers close to home or job; the stigma felt by the middle class in sending children to former WPA centers or places closely resembling them; and the high cost of care for working-class mothers. That this state of affairs was partly intentional is asserted by Sheila Rothman in *Woman's Proper Place* (New York, 1980) who notes that in 1942 even the Children's Bureau opposed locating day-care centers near defense plants because "they might be too convenient, outlive the emergency, and encourage women to stay at work."

Historians have also contended that women willingly returned to the home after the war. A large number of women in Michigan, Clive maintains, decided against future employment if their husbands could support them or if men needed work. Little complaint existed in Lowell, Miller says, about the temporary nature of jobs; most women were either content or were resigned to returning home and recreating old economic hierarchies. Hartmann reaches the same conclusion, somewhat circuitously: while admitting that her evidence is generally drawn from male advice in popular and social scientific journals, she nevertheless concludes that women, either out of guilt or because of prior social conditioning, probably agreed to resume their old domestic role.

A closer reading of these articles, however, provides another interpretation. For one, these assertions by the authors are unsupported. For example, Hartmann believes that some of the prescriptions by veterans that women remain home may well have been actual descriptions of the roles their wives were assuming, but nowhere does she cite the opinions of the wives. If anything, her evidence points in another direction. That government, social, scientific, and popular literature frequently called on women to give up their independence in part reflects the concern of society that women had other intentions, a concern Hartmann herself admits existed. Nor was this concern unfounded. Specialists attributed exceptionally high divorce rates after the war in part to the separate existence experienced by both parties during the war, a subject discussed at counseling sessions and psychiatric interviews with veterans and their families. (This is noted in Rebecca Greene's ''The Role of the Psychiatrist in World War II,'' unpublished dissertation, 1976.) But one does not need to look at divorce to find such evidence. A survey of women by the Women's Bureau in 1945 revealed that 75 per cent of those working wanted to continue to work after the War; 60 per cent of former housewives, the group expected to be most conventional, also wanted to continue work.

In ''Women's Place is in the War'' (*Women in America,* ed. Carol Ruth Berkin and Mary Beth Norton, Boston, 1979, 342–359) Leila Rupp finds that wartime propaganda and working women's actual interests diverged. Although Office of War Information (OWI) propaganda from 1942–1945 encouraged women to work out of patriotism (thus temporarily) and to retain their femininity and housekeeping skills so they could easily return home, the women themselves did not see their work as temporary. According to letters from specially selected, ''able and unbiased'' female observers to the OWI, women workers believed they were working for ''income'' and ''out of dissatisfaction with housewifery,'' not just because of the war. The articles on Lowell and Michigan support Rupp's position, for the vast bulk of the women they studied were working in industry to support their families. Nevertheless, a distinction can be drawn between the interests of employed middle-class and working-class women. As Paddy Quick observes in ''Rosie the Riveter: Myths and Realities'' (*Radical America,* IX, 1975, 115–132) many women had no choice but to work. Both during and after the war economic necessity compelled working class women to work, even when they had to accept lower paying, less skilled jobs afterwards. Quick notes a second reason why ''Rosie the Riveter'' continued employment. During and after World War II, the economy generated consumer durable products such as washing machines, processed foods, refrigerators, wash and wear clothes, and vacuums, which saved the employed woman time at home. The rise in the manufacture of durable goods also created a greater demand for female labor. Among the women who persisted in the factories after the war were black women who had left their jobs as domestics. A third reason why working-class women continued to work was a growing female interest, generated by the war, in working for wages.

Thus, quite a few of the articles show that neither middle nor working-class women were interested in returning to domesticity during or after the war. What, then, was the source of ''public opinion'' alluded to by a few historians in favor of women returning home? Rupp answers that it was men, the male correspondents in the OWI collection, who were the ones worried that "women might replace them in the labor force or depress wages or that the employment of some might destroy family life."

Women not only expressed opinions against resuming their lives in the home, but took action. Contrary to the assertion of Clive, Gabin documents quite a number of cases brought before the appeals committee of the International Executive Board, various leaders of the International Union, and the Women's Bureau from 1945-54. These appeals concerned lower pay for the same work as men; unfair transfers owing to separate seniority lists; or physical, sexual, or verbal harassment. The purpose of these protested actions was either to drive women out or to prevent them from filing grievances. While many of the complaints Gabin refers to came from women dismissed because of marriage, engagement, or pregnancy, single women were not exempt: contracts stipulated that they be dismissed after married women, but before laying off any men, and that men be re-hired first. Gabin concludes by noting that these appeals represent only the "tip of the iceberg," since local union officials harassed women to stop them from bringing their cases before the International and did not inform them of the appeal process. A study of the appeals from workers to management has not yet been made. Clive and Miller might have reassessed their conclusions about female acquiescence had they studied the appeal process in other unions in Michigan and Lowell. Perhaps a weakness in their articles is that they tend to generalize about the effects of World War II by concentrating on 1945-1946, when in reality many of the repercussions did not become evident until the early 1950s.

Another way to evaluate progress for the American woman in World War II is to compare it to that in other countries during the war. A review of the periodical literature shows that women in the United States fared better than some and worse than others, and the primary factor in the evolution of the female role in other countries was not necessity but cultural norm. In "Women's Emancipation and the Recruitment of Women into the Canadian Labour Force in World War II" (*Canadian Historical Papers*, 1976, 141-173), Ruth Pierson shows that a more receptive attitude in Canada than in the United States toward women working played a greater role in determining policy than the exigencies of war. Although Canada played a less strategic role than the United States in the war, it developed a more flexible employment policy for women. Canada registered women for conscription; developed flexible programs of part-time work, night shifts, temporary three-month stints, and day-care next to the plant; and introduced tax incentives for husbands with working wives. All these measures were designed to facilitate the employment of wives and mothers.

In contrast, the norms of Japan and Germany were much more conservative and female labor was less used, despite more serious labor shortages. In "Women and War in Japan, 1937-1945" (*American Historical Review,* LXXX, 1975, 913-934) Thomas Havens remarks that although single Japanese women (16 to 25 years old) were registered as early as November 1941, the government did nothing to call them up. There was some belated rhetoric in late 1943, but even then government propaganda was more interested in promoting marriage than getting women to work. When the labor supply fell even further in 1944, Japan conducted some drives to get women for the aircraft industry. Yet marriage continued to be encouraged and single women were excused if needed at home. In August, 1944 Japan imposed heavy fines on women who refused to work in industry; still, massive evasions testify to the total absence of enforcement. Where then did Japan get its additional labor? Havens points to the transfer of men from non-essential to essential industries and the mobilization of male students and old men.

The contrast between the United States and Japan is striking. While the total number of working women in the United States increased 50 per cent during the war, it rose only 10 per cent in Japan; and while the upsurge was particularly apparent in American industry, Japanese women working in factories actually declined from 25 per cent in 1930 to 24 per cent during the height of the war. What accounts for the difference? According to Havens, on the eve of the war, virtually all women in Japan who worked outside the home were single, while married women who "worked" were wives of farmers working in the fields. This tradition continued during the war, with registration for single women only. Added to this was the assumption that the most important role a woman could perform for the state was to be a mother. The government set up matchmaking agencies and marriage counseling centers, encouraged private companies to pay baby bonuses to workers, and lent wedding clothes to poor couples who could not afford ceremonies. The Japanese War Minister's interest in eugenics led to the outlawing of birth control, sterilization of the insane, and scholarships to families with ten children or more. (Still, by the end of the war, with industry crippled by American bombing and food scarce, births declined at least 15 per cent.)

Germany was less restrictive in using female workers than Japan, but it too lagged behind the United States. In "Women, Class, and Mobilization in Nazi Germany" (*Science and Society,* XLIII, 1979, 51-69) Leila Rupp states that while the American female labor force rose 32 per cent from 1941–1945, that of Germany rose only 1 per cent between 1939 and 1944, testimony to the resistance of the government to hiring women. As early as 1939, a decree was established empowering the state to "conscript individuals for work of national importance," but this was rarely invoked. For the next four years, Hitler opposed women working, until January, 1943, when the labor crunch persuaded him to order the registration of all women aged 17 to 49. Even so, throughout the war middle and upper-class women frequently evaded work, whereas working-class women were forced to work because of a 1939 ruling that persons who were employed before the war could be conscripted.

The question Rupp poses is why middle and upper-class females were so inadequately employed. Although acknowledging that Hitler and other Nazi leaders were ideologically opposed to women working, she argues that failure to mobilize was mostly a result of the lack of response from women to the demands of the regime. It was not the bourgeois values of Hitler per se, but the attitudes and actions of women who were well off, which accounted for the resistance to employment. Referring to reports by official observers to the Security Service (SD) of the SS, which collected information throughout the war on public opinion, Rupp concludes that the reluctance of middle-class women to work was the result of the loss of dependency allowances for married women who worked; inadequate daycare; a shortage of professional and white collar jobs compatible with middle-class status; inequitable pay; and a general belief that women should not work when their husbands could support them. She might have added, as she did in her article "Mother of the *Volk*" (*Signs*, III, 1977, 362–379), that the Nazis gave loans to couples about to be married, provided the women promised not to work until the loan was repaid. In addition, the reports to the SD confirm the resentment of the lower class: women in factories were jealous of middle and upper-class females staying at home; and their husbands resented risking their lives at the front while bureaucrats, safe and sound, could be catered to by full-time housewives.

The implication of Rupp's thesis, that the response of German women primarily determined their low employment, is as conservative as those that explain the inadequate use of American day-care in World War II and the return of American women to the home. For in all three cases, placing the blame on female attitudes implies that the state could have done little else. Nowhere does she say how many reports were filed with the SD, how the objectivity of observers was determined, what kind of questions were asked of women and what procedures were used to elicit answers. Perhaps the questions were chosen and the phrasing selected so as to elicit a lack of interest in working on the part of middle-class women, for then working-class women would not blame the Nazi regime for favoring the more privileged classes, a criticism going to the heart of Nazi ideology of equality.

There is a second problem in Rupp's thesis. It is hard to accept the notion that no group within middle and upper-class women believed that women (single and married) should work. This is especially so since, in "Mother of the *Volk*," Rupp notes that during the early 1930s some of the leading female Nazi ideologues, such as Irmgard Reichenau, maintained that "talented women with careers would make better mothers than full-time mothers." It is true that, by the mid-1930s, this kind of thinking had retreated in favor of the middle position that the good Nazi woman did whatever the state wanted, and the more conservative one, that the greatest thing a woman could do was to bear an Aryan child. Still, it is hard to imagine that it died out totally. Or, if it did, may it not be that such an evaporation testified more to the repressiveness of the Nazi regime, or at least to the efficacy of propaganda by Hitler and other male ideologues, than to middle and upper-class female opinion? Furthermore, Rupp herself notes that one of the main reasons that middle-class women were not interested was the inadequacy of state facilities for working mothers and economic disincentives for married women. Perhaps state policy—repression, propaganda, welfare—was the horse and the opinions of middle and upper-class women were the cart, and not the reverse. (A final interesting note is that American propaganda, according to Trey, urged women to work by threatening that if the United States were defeated, women would experience the same "enslavement" as their German sisters.)

This review has shown that with respect to the changing role of women, the United States in World War II took a middle position: more advances were made than in the totalitarian countries, but fewer than in Canada. Nevertheless, questions remain. For instance, while American literature during World War II discussed juvenile delinquency, recent historians have not covered this topic or, for that matter, the family in general. In "Women Workers in the Second World War" (*Capital and Class*, I, 1977, 27–42) Penny Summerfield examines the contradiction that existed in Great Britain during the emergency of war between working to full capacity and a good family life; a similar article might be written for the United States. Nor is there periodical literature on the role of the soldier's or officer's wife, a subject of interest in contemporary sociological journals. (One might, for example, look at articles by Nancy L. Goldman, M. Duncan Stanton, Ellwyn Stoddard and Claude E. Cabanillas in *The Social Psychology of Military Service,* London, 1976.) One unpublished paper by Heather Frazier and John O'Sullivan, "Forgotten Women of World War II" (Women and Power Conference, College Park, Maryland, 1977), describes the effects of war on the wives of conscientious objectors, but this is only a beginning. In the last few years, articles have also been written on the volunteer army and on the role of women in particular (including the entire summer 1978 issue of *Armed Forces and Society*). Although the origins of a female military force can be traced to the world wars, little has been written on World War II. Susan M. Hartmann has an article on "The Impact of War on Sex Roles: Women in the Military Service" in *Clio Was a Woman* (Washington, D.C., 1980) but this has just been published.

A final point needs to be made. Rupp's valuable distinction between the role and attitudes of different classes of German women has not been made in a similar fashion for the United States. Quick's comparison of "bourgeois" and working-class women is done much too cursorily. With the exception of Chafe, most of the literature surveyed has concentrated on the working class. There is room for additional articles on the middle-class woman. Rupp's analysis of the OWI correspondence with housewives and social workers is a start, but we need more accounts of professional and white-collar women during the War.

Rebecca S. Greene is a member of The Institute for Research in History.

Journals Consulted

American Historical Review • Armed Forces and Society • Canadian Historical Papers • Capital and Class • Feminist Studies • Journal of American History • Journal of Family History • Journal of Interdisciplinary History • Journal of Social History • Journal of Social Issues • Journal of Southern History • Labor History • Military Affairs • New England Quarterly • Peace and Change • Politics and Society • Prologue • Public Interest • Radical America • Review of Radical Political Economics • Science and Society • Signs • Women's Studies.

THE UNITED STATES:
THE MILITARY, WAR, AND FOREIGN POLICY

Thomas R. English

A decade ago, Allan Millett proclaimed that military history had gone "over the top" to reach scholarly acceptance and academic respectability ("American Military History: Over the Top," *The State of American History,* Herbert J. Bass, ed., Chicago, 1970). That judgment turned out to be premature. While Millett correctly observed that military history had been "demilitarized" in the sense that its practitioners no longer write exclusively operational and strategic history for military men, liberal academics have continued to confound the military historian and the militarist. One result of this attitude is that articles dealing with the military, and especially military operations, are not welcome in many journals; work in military history tends to be found in the field's own journal, *Military Affairs,* and in books. Ironically, publishers have found that books on military history have a larger market among the public than virtually any other field of historical writing.

Millett also urged historians of the military to do more work in the field of national security policy, exploring the interrelationship of the military, the conduct of war, and the conduct of foreign policy. World War II and the Cold War had done much to interest civilian military historians in national security problems. Millett's urging came at a time when some of the most exciting work in American history was being done in national security affairs. In 1971, the second volume appeared of William Braisted's monumental work, *The United States Navy in the Pacific* (Austin, Texas). Two years later, Richard Challener published his study of military and naval attitudes and influence, *Admirals, Generals, and American Foreign Policy, 1989-1914* (Princeton). Perhaps the high-point of this approach came with the publication in 1973 of *Pearl Harbor as History: Japanese-American Relations, 1931-1941* (New York), the product of a 1969 conference held in Japan. This work included papers by both Japanese and American scholars on all aspects of Japanese-American relations, from military and diplomatic contacts to finances and foreign trade.

Just as the national security approach seemed to reach its peak, however, some military historians began to call for a return to operational histories. In "A Modest Plea for Drums and Trumpets" (*Military Affairs,* XXXIX, 1975, 71-74) Dennis Showalter reminded his colleagues that armies have a purpose, to wage war, and should be studied with that purpose in mind. Moreover, Showalter argued, an emphasis on the social setting in which military forces exist can lead to dangerous distortions. Military, not social factors, best explain the Roman defeat of the Greek phalanx at Pydna in 168 B.C. and the Austrian victory over the Sardinians at Custoza in 1848. Seconding Showalter's call was Russell Weigley in the introduction to *New Dimensions in Military History* (San Rafael, California, 1975).

War and the Nation-State

The modern study of war and policy began with the work of the German historian and military philosopher Karl von Clausewitz, whose most famous work, *On War,* appeared posthumously in 1831. Peter Moody's superb article, "Clausewitz and the Fading Dialectic of War" (*World Politics,* XXXI, 1979, 417-433) relates the theory of war to the historical institution of the nation-state. Clausewitz spoke of war in dialectical terms: the theoretical war of unlimited violence, and the actual conduct of war in which state policy controls the use of force. Moody points out that Clausewitz studied war just when it was moving beyond the control of the nation-state, toward the modern phenomenon of total war in which the roles of soldier and non-combatant civilian are no longer distinct. Moody's special point is that the growth of liberalism, democracy, and nationalism during the 19th century was intimately connected with the development of total war. Knowing what total war means, the democratic society of today must overcome its liberal aversion to the study of war in order to evolve means to control it.

Michael Howard, the foremost historian of the theory of war, treats this topic in some recent articles. In "War and the Nation-State" (*Daedalus,* CVIII, 1979, 101-110) Howard pursues much the same theme as Moody. The first and primary function of the nation-state was and is the use of military power, since without such power the independent nation-state may cease to exist. But when the nation-state first appeared, in 17th and 18th-century Europe, the prince and the government controlled military policy. The period 1776-1918 saw a fusion of the people, the prince, and the government, a fusion that led to total war, but events since 1918 have tended to separate the people once again from the military and the government. In this new situation, states may prove reluctant to use force even when their vital interests are threatened. Howard reminds us that the "disintegration of decadent states" can lead to war as much as "the aggression of strong ones," and thus the current separation of peoples and governments has created a situation conducive to war. Even worse, according to Howard, is the proliferation of terrorist groups; the loss by national authorities of their monopoly on the legitimate use of force can only lead to chaos.

Howard states the same theme in "The Forgotten Dimensions of Strategy" (*Foreign Affairs,* LVII, 1979, 975-986). In this article he argues that governments must take responsibility for uniting the people and the government, the best way being not through propaganda and manipulation but through an honest statement of policy. This unity is necessary, Howard says, because there remains a very real possibility that war in the modern world will be conventional rather than nuclear, resembling in many ways the wars of the first half of this century. If so, a society must be able to mobilize all of its resources, but that can only be done if the people and the government are united in purpose.

Security without War

As both Howard and Moody suggest, liberal societies are uncomfortable with theoretical justifications of war as an instrument of national policy, perhaps because they see a lingering flavor of immorality in the idea. This discomfort has been reinforced by the Vietnam experience, when such ideas seemed to be directing national policy. But examining history for successful attempts to avoid war while maintaining national security can be discouraging. One of the most famous efforts to avoid war was Jefferson's Embargo Act of 1808, which halted all American trade in an effort to force Britain and France to respect the right of the United States to trade with both sides in the Continental struggle. Richard Mannix examines the issue of "Gallatin, Jefferson and the Embargo of 1808" (*Diplomatic History,* III, 1979, 151-172) and finds that it was not Jefferson's Embargo at all. Jefferson did not conceive the idea, did not support it strongly, and in fact avoided having anything very much to do with it, leaving everything to the originator of the idea, Secretary of the Treasury Albert Gallatin. After the *Chesapeake* incident of 1807, in which the British frigate *Leopard* attacked the American frigate *Chesapeake* and impressed some of her crew, Jefferson expected war. By the time a special session of Congress had assembled, however, the lateness of the year and the rapid fading of public outrage convinced him to seek other means than war to pressure Britain. When the unpopularity of the Embargo became clear, Gallatin became a convenient scapegoat for all concerned. It became "Jefferson's Embargo" only after his retirement, when the War of 1812 had come and gone and Jefferson was willing to write letters asserting that, if only it had been maintained longer, the Embargo could have helped avoid war.

Probably the most famous international attempt to prevent war was the Kellogg-Briand Pact of 1928, generally scorned by diplomatic and military historians as a symbol of the muddled idealism of the 1920s. This was the treaty in which the signatory powers promised never to use war as an instrument of national policy, except in self defense. Harold Josephson tries to rehabilitate the treaty and its importance in his article "Outlawing War: Internationalism and the Pact of Paris" (*Diplomatic History,* III, 1979, 377–390). He argues that many of the Pact's principles are now part of American foreign policy. Unfortunately, the illustrations he chooses, such as the Nuremberg trials of officers accused of conspiring to wage aggressive war, or the United Nations Charter, seem to have suffered over the years. At Nuremberg, generals and admirals sat in the dock, but after the My Lai massacre the chain of command's responsibility stopped with a lieutenant.

In fact, American attitudes toward "Internationalism" and collective security have always been more ambiguous than Josephson indicates. Some historians have seen the "Stimson Doctrine," the policy of non-recognition of the Japanese conquest of Manchuria in 1931, as an effort by the Secretary of State to put the United States, in cooperation with the League of Nations, at the vanguard in opposing aggression. Much nearer the mark is Gary Ostrower's study of "Secretary of State Stimson and the League" (*The Historian,* XLI, 1979, 467–482). Ostrower demonstrates that Stimson was not a consistent supporter of American involvement with the League. At the time of the Japanese invasion of Manchuria in 1931, Stimson veered back and forth between cooperation with the League and an independent American policy. Indeed, he mirrored the confused attitudes of the country, and not until he left office and wrote his memoirs did he become a total convert to collective security.

War, Alliances and Diplomacy

When diplomats fail, war may result, and in the century of total war the world has been drawn up in competing alliances. The Grand Alliance of World War II has often been called the most successful military coalition in history. Perhaps so, but one of the major contributions of New Left historiography has been to show that the members of the alliance did not always work in harmony. There were many controversial strategic decisions, as well as constant jockeying for postwar advantage. With the door thus opened, other scholars are exploring the strains within the alliance.

Thomas Hachey breaks new ground with his article "Walter White and the American Negro Soldier in World War II: A Diplomatic Dilemma for Britain" (*Phylon*, XXXIX, 1978, 241–249). White, who was the Executive Secretary of the National Association for the Advancement of Colored People and thus a powerful American political figure, went to England to investigate the conditions of black troops. Many reports had reached him that black troops were suffering discrimination in the American armed forces, and the British leaders wanted his trip to focus on those problems, rather than similar incidents between black Americans and British citizens. Thus when White sought a meeting with Winston Churchill and the foreign secretary, the British declined. Their problem was to find a means to deflect White's anger, in order to avoid a diplomatic insult with racial overtones. Fortunately for them, they could blame the U.S. Embassy, which had failed to make any preliminary arrangements for such meetings. There is a growing literature on blacks in the armed forces, and Hachey is to be complimented for placing that service in a larger context.

A policy that was intended to avoid strains within the alliance was the "unconditional surrender" formula, the subject of Michael Balfour's "The Origins of the Formula: Unconditional Surrender in World War II" (*Armed Forces and Society*, V, 1979, 281–301). Contrary to President Franklin D. Roosevelt's own account of the origin of the policy—that it just "popped into" his mind during a press conference—unconditional surrender had been under discussion in a State Department committee since the start of the war. Balfour goes on to discuss some of the arguments for and against the policy, concluding that its advantages far outweighed the disadvantages, most of which are based on counterfactual arguments about the Nazi resistance. The primary advantage was that the unconditional surrender policy would cement the alliance more firmly, since no member would consider German offers of a separate peace. It was especially intended to reassure the Soviets, though in this respect it never entirely succeeded. In any case, Roosevelt was firmly committed to the policy and refused to reconsider it.

The demand for unconditional surrender is often interpreted as one indication of the unity of the American people during World War II. Richard Steele tries to change that image in his article "American Popular

Opinion and the War Against Germany: The Issue of Negotiated Peace, 1942" (*Journal of American History*, LXV, 1978, 704–723). Steele, arguing that the country was far from united (and its leaders knew it), notes that "solidarity during the war meant little more than majority acceptance of the course of events," rather than a "public commitment to the principles, policies and persons directing national affairs." What he overlooks is that he has posed separate questions in that sentence, because support for the principles might co-exist with indifference toward the persons. Moreover, public opinion polling in the 1940s, on which he bases his conclusions, was far less reliable than today.

That is not to say that the Roosevelt administration was indifferent to criticism. In a separate article, "Franklin Delano Roosevelt and his Foreign Policy Critics" (*Political Science Quarterly*, XCIV, 1978, 15–32), Steele establishes that the administration used a now familiar tactic against its enemies—identifying them with the nation's enemies. Commenting on Steele's article, Arthur Schlesinger, Jr. defends Roosevelt in the same issue, but there seems little doubt that information was sometimes managed to protect the administration from domestic criticism. To cite an example (not mentioned in Steele's article), the embarrassing details of the battle of Savo Island, a disastrous naval defeat suffered by the Allies off Guadalcanal in 1942, were still classified in the early 1950s and could not be revealed ten years later in the television series *Victory at Sea*.

The New Left's concern with American economic expansion during the war, often at the expense of Britain, appears in Lloyd Beecher, Jr.'s study of "The Second World War and U.S. Politico-Economic Expansion: The Case of Liberia, 1938–1945" (*Diplomatic History*, III, 1979, 391–412) and Phillip Baram's "Undermining the British: Department of State Policies in Egypt and the Suez Canal Before and During World War II" (*The Historian*, XLI, 1978, 631–649). However, both articles fall into the New Left penchant for dwelling on policies that largely failed or involved regions of secondary importance, and trying to escalate them into the major concerns of U.S. policy makers. A more successful New Left approach is Lawrence Wittner's examination of "American Policy Toward Greece During World War II" (*Diplomatic History*, III, 1979, 129–150), which shows the United States, Britain, and the Soviet Union combining to thwart the ambitions of the leftist Greek guerillas, even though it eventually meant using force against an anti-Nazi resistance movement.

The New Left does not accept that the expansion of U.S. security interests had any legitimacy, even in the years before and during the Second World War. But to look at that expansion from a national security point of view one can turn to Gerald Haines' article, "The Roosevelt Administration Interprets the Monroe Doctrine" (*Australian Journal of Politics and History*, XXIV, 1978, 332-345). According to Haines, the administration began thinking in terms of hemispheric security in the 1930s, but it was only wartime developments that convinced the policy makers to intervene in Europe and Asia. The Monroe Doctrine changed from being a justification of policy to an embarrassment. That the United States still intended to dominate the hemisphere, in spite of increasing talk of "multilateralism," can be seen in American strategic planning involving Latin America, as discussed by John Child in "From 'Color' to 'Rainbow'; U. S. Strategic Planning for Latin America, 1919-1954" (*Journal of Interamerican Studies and World Affairs*, XXI, 1979, 233-260).

The Origins of the Cold War

The early years of the Cold War remain a favorite topic for historians of national security policy. George Quester tries a new approach to the question of responsibility in his article, "Origins of the Cold War: Some Clues from Public Opinion" (*Political Science Quarterly*, XCIII, 1979, 647-664). He concludes that public opinion in Europe and America moved from trusting the Soviet Union to belligerence, but the movement came in response to Soviet actions. From this evidence, Quester concludes that the West was in fact pacific and the Soviets belligerent, and thus the Soviets are more responsible for the start of the Cold War. One cannot help but wonder, though, whether this reaction resulted from successful news management by the U.S. political leadership, rather than from the aggressive intent of Soviet policy.

Three different historians have recently urged us to consider the importance of personalities in the developing Cold War. Larry Bland examines "Averill Harriman, the Russians and the Origins of the Cold War in Europe, 1943-1945" (*Australian Journal of Politics and History*, XXIII, 1977, 403-416) and finds that Harriman was important in changing American policy; but the implication exists that the more important changes were shifts among policy makers in Washington. The same mixed message is found in Elizabeth Kimball MacLean's article on "Joseph E. Davies and Soviet-American Relations, 1941-43" (*Diplomatic History*, IV, 1980, 73-94). Davies enjoyed the confidence of Soviet officials to a high degree, and as a result Roosevelt employed him as a liaison officer with the Soviet Embassy in Washington from 1941 to 1943. But when American policy changed after the Potsdam Conference of 1945, Davies lost his influence.

Wilson Mixcamble ("Anthony Eden and the Truman-Molotov Conversations, April 1945" [*Diplomatic History*, II, 1978, 167–180]) looks at a specific incident, the Truman-Molotov conversation of April 23, 1945, and finds that Eden arranged it, hoping that a personal meeting could solve several disputes with the Soviets. Instead, of course, the meeting backfired and may have convinced the Soviets that the Truman administration was completely hostile.

Many of the most important postwar American policies originated in the Truman years. Lawrence Wittner examines "The Truman Doctrine and the Defense of Freedom" (*Diplomatic History*, IV, 1980, 161–188) and finds that there was no connection between the two. In order to defeat Communist subversion in Greece, American officials were willing to tolerate police-state measures of the harshest kind. In an article difficult to summarize, Scott Jackson explores the roots of policy in "Prologue to the Marshall Plan: The Origins of the American Commitment for a European Recovery Program" (*Journal of American History*, LXV, 1979, 1043–1068). It is a noteworthy article because it does an excellent job of demonstrating the complex nature of policy making, as Jackson shows the many influences that combined to produce George Marshall's aid plan for Europe.

Walter Poole notes in his "From Conciliation to Containment: The Joint Chiefs of Staff and the Coming of the Cold War, 1945–1946" (*Military Affairs*, XLII, 1978, 12–16) that the Joint Chiefs of Staff (JCS) were not in the forefront of policy making at the start of the Cold War. Their advice tended to be offered in response to requests from other departments. But when it was offered, a JCS opinion carried great weight, with the prestige of America's recent victory adding to the their influence. Poole goes on to demonstrate that the JCS did not urge an aggressive policy of opposing Soviet policy in eastern Europe; rather, they assumed that the United States would mediate what were essentially Anglo-Soviet disputes. During the course of 1945, the Chiefs increasingly came to view the Soviet Union as an expansionist power that threatened U.S. security. Poole adds that the JCS seemed to have reached this conclusion earlier than the State Department did; not until the Soviets attempted to control northern Iran in 1946 did the diplomats accept the military view of Soviet policy. In July of that year, the JCS formulated an "interdepartmental definition" of the containment policy, but to their minds this policy was a "defensive reaction, not an offensive thrust.

The Jackson and Poole articles both indicate that American policy was the product of many groups, individuals, and interests, and as a result it could be flexible. Lorraine Lees follows the same theme in her study of "The American Decision to Assist Tito, 1948–1949" (*Diplomatic History*, II, 1978, 407–422). She finds that in spite of a history of strained relations with Tito during and immediately after the war, American policy makers jumped at the chance to send aid, hoping it would lead to similar developments throughout Eastern Europe. As she concludes, it is hard to understand why the United States could be pragmatic in its dealings with Tito yet at the same time so rigid in its reactions to Communism in East Asia.

The United States and East Asia

The question of pragmatism applies to Robert McMahon's article on "Anglo-American Diplomacy and the Reoccupation of the Netherlands East Indies" (*Diplomatic History*, II, 1978, 1–24). Both the United States and Britain sought to aid the Dutch in their reoccupation of Indonesia. But when the independence movement led by Sukarno seemed on the verge of victory, both Britain and the United States were able to adjust their policy to the new reality. American mediation helped to create a genuinely independent Indonesia; here Washington was flexible. Yet in China, during and after the war, American policy was far more rigid. John Miller's article, "The Chiang-Stilwell Conflict, 1942–1944" (*Military Affairs,* XLIII, 1979, 59–62), repeats the familiar story while adding nothing new.

Far more interesting is Steven Levine's "A New Look at American Mediation in the Chinese Civil War: The Marshall Mission and Manchuria" (*Diplomatic History,* III, 1979, 349–376). From December 1945 to January 1947, Marshall was in China trying to arrange a cease-fire in the Civil War and a coalition government. Since he did not succeed in these objects, most historians view the mission as a failure. Levine sees Marshall's mission as a failure only in terms of events within China, since it did not unify the nation nor end the Civil War. But its real purpose was grounded in global strategy: the United States wanted to prevent Soviet expansion into China and especially Manchuria. In these terms, he argues, the Marshall mission was a success.

The growing American involvement in the Far East is shown by James Matray in his "An End to Indifference: America's Korean Policy During World War II" (*Diplomatic History,* II, 1978, 181–196). Matray finds that the Roosevelt administration, realizing that the strategically significant Korean peninsula would be important to peace after the war, strove for an international trusteeship that would create an independent, non-Communist

Korea. The less desirable alternative was to commit American troops to guarantee Korean independence. In either case, America's historic indifference to Korea was at an end.

In another article on Korea, John Edward Wiltz re-examines "Truman and MacArthur; The Wake Island Meeting" (*Military Affairs*, XLII, 1978, 169-176). Most descriptions of this meeting, he argues, are based on memoirs, especially Truman's, and these are not reliable sources. Using what amount to a secretary's minutes, Wiltz concludes that there was no military purpose to the meeting. Although MacArthur did say that the Chinese would not intervene in Korea, the real reason for the meeting was to put President Truman back on the front pages before the fall elections. James Matray follows up his earlier study of American policy in Korea with an article on "Truman's Plan for Victory: National Self-Determination and the Thirty-eighth Parallel Decision in Korea" (*Journal of American History*, LXVI, 1979, 314-333). He finds that Truman's decision to order American forces across the 38th parallel was an effort to force a resolution of the Korean predicament that had defied policy makers for five years. The conquest of North Korea would unite the nation and give it the opportunity of national self-determination. This had been the primary aim of American policy in Korea since World War II.

Russell Buhite also follows the development of American involvement in the Far East in his article "Major Interests: American Policy toward China, Taiwan, and Korea, 1945-1950" (*Pacific Historical Review*, XLVII, 1978, 425-451). Before the war, Buhite argues, American interests could be divided into either "vital" or "peripheral." But the years after 1945 saw a new category emerge, which Buhite terms "major interests," areas that were worth substantial American involvement short of military commitments. The change occurred because global strategy changed: the United States was seeking to become the major power in the Far East while also blocking Soviet expansion in the area. The Korean War demonstrated that the distinctions among types of interests were blurring in response to events, and the Vietnam War was the ultimate product of this blurring. American policy makers could no longer distinguish vital interests that must be defended by force from peripheral interests that could be compromised without damaging security. Gary Hess reaches an opposite conclusion in his article, "The First American Commitment in Indochina: The Acceptance of the 'Bao Dai Solution,' 1950" (*Diplomatic History*, II, 1978, 331-350). Hess argues that the United States had a clear policy. It sought the peaceful and orderly transfer of power from colonial powers to Western-oriented native leaders, a policy that worked in the Philippines and Indonesia but failed in Vietnam where the Communists led the nationalist movement. The result was a dilemma that American policy makers could not solve, either in 1950 or later.

The Vietnam War

A more recent case where politics and diplomacy influenced the conduct of military operations was the Vietnam war. Since the end of American participation in the war, Vietnam has been an increasingly popular subject for historical writing. Peter Braestrup has surveyed the literature for the *Wilson Quarterly* (II, 1978, 178-187) in his article "Vietnam as History." A survey of a different type is Russell Fifield's "Vietnam: A Unique American Experience" (*The Yale Review*, XLVIII, 1979, 161-175), Fifield presents an overview of Vietnam and compares it with other American wars. He finds that while Korea presented some similarities, no other war in U.S. experience was anything like Vietnam. Among the distinguishing features Fifield finds is the extent of political control of military operations. This is certainly a debatable conclusion, since there was nothing unique about such control in the American military experience. More accurately, he discusses other distinguishing features, such as the effort to use military operations to send political messages through the escalation or de-escalation of military activity; and he rightly notes that Vietnam was the first televised war. Fifield ends with the hope that Vietnam will always remain an aberration in U.S. military history.

Another overview of Vietnam takes a far less optimistic course. Harvey DeWeerd examines "Strategic Decision Making: Vietnam, 1965-1968" (*The Yale Review*, LXVII, 1978, 481-492). He finds that machinery for rational policy-making on national security issues existed throughout the period of his study, but that it failed to produce rational policy. The reasons are two. First, the machinery did not operate, because President Lyndon Johnson chose to make policy with the aid of his political advisers and for narrowly political reasons. Secondly, once the policy was in place, it turned out that the machinery did not include any method for continuing strategic debate or for the reexamination of the policy that such debate would have involved. Accordingly, the objectives established for our involvement went unchallenged, even when they proved to be hopelessly optimistic; the result was the surprise of the Tet offensive of 1968, which forced the United States to re-evaluate its role in Vietnam. That reconsideration led to modified objectives and the beginning of what the Nixon administration was later to call "Vietnamization." DeWeerd concludes gloomily that there is little evidence that Johnson's successors have drawn the proper lessons from the decision-making failures of the Vietnam war tragedy.

A specific example of flawed strategic planning is the subject of Richard Schultz's article "Breaking the Will of the Enemy During the Vietnam War: The Operationalization of the Cost-Benefit Model of Counterinsurgency Warfare" (*Journal of Peace Research,* XV, 1978, 109–130). According to Schultz, the American effort in Vietnam failed because of theoretical and operational problems inherent in its chosen strategy. The United States correctly realized that it was necessary to separate the insurgents from the populace which provided them with recruits and supplies. But the Johnson administration chose the cost-benefit or "suppressive" strategy, trying to use force to control behavior rather than attempting to win popular support through social reform. This approach was based on a model of the population as rational decision makers; when the costs of supporting the insurgents became too high, the populace would shift to supporting the government. Thus it was a central assumption of this strategy that individuals and groups behave rationally at all times and in all situations, calculating costs and benefits. That assumption proved to be wrong in Vietnam, as might have been expected of an assumption based on Western economic theory. Another side of American policy was the strategy of attrition that guided military operations, again as part of the cost-benefit approach. But the United States never had the ability to impose so many casualties on the enemy that reinforcements would have been inadequate. By its own calculations, the Defense Department should have known that the enemy could replace losses without serious problems, given an American force level of 500,000 men. Thus American strategy contained flaws of a theoretical and operational nature, flaws that led almost inevitably to defeat.

Another study gives us an idea of how difficult it may be to learn any lessons from Vietnam. Ole Holst and James Rosenau did extensive surveying of American leaders to study "Vietnam, Consensus, and the Belief Systems of American Leaders" (*World Politics,* XXXII, 1979, 1–56). They found, not surprisingly, that Vietnam had shattered the existing foreign policy consensus. Moreover, the current views of the leaders surveyed seemed to hinge on their interpretation of the lessons of Vietnam. Yet there was very little agreement about those lessons. Holst and Rosenau identify seven distinct groups in the post-Vietnam positions, with those at either end of the spectrum, the critics and supporters, each representing about one-third of the respondents. In such circumstances, they conclude, it is hard to see how any new foreign policy consensus can be established.

It may take some dramatic international developments to bring about a new foreign policy consensus. One can only wonder if events in Iran and Afghanistan are supplying exactly those circumstances, especially in the context of the 1980 presidential contest.

Some of the dangers of trying to write contemporary history can be found in another article by Russell Fifield, "The Liquidation of a War: The United States and Vietnam (*Asia Quarterly,* 1978, 209-228). Fifield begins by defining the period of "liquidation" of the war as the period following the fall of Saigon to North Vietnamese troops in 1975. Much of what he wrote about the course of diplomatic relations between Hanoi and Washington has turned out to be overly optimistic. There has been no generous settlement of issues, nor has the United States chosen to grant reconstruction aid to Hanoi. Current developments in Indochina—Vietnamese control of Cambodia and attacks on Thailand—discourage any possible reconciliation.

Military Operations and Diplomacy

An interesting trend has been to examine the diplomatic impact of specific military operations. One such article is James Carr's study of "The Battle of New Orleans and the Treaty of Ghent" (*Diplomatic History,* II, 1978, 273-282). The battle occurred after the conclusion of the peace treaty that ended the War of 1812, but many historians have argued that the battle still had an important influence. Had the United States lost, this argument runs, Britain might have declined to ratify the treaty in an attempt to take advantage of the victory. Carr's research leads to a very different conclusion. He finds that in fact the British had already ratified the treaty, and the ratification traveled to the United States on the same ship as the treaty itself. The reason for this prompt action was that the British did not trust the United States, which had already established a reputation for failing to ratify agreements. In 1814, Britain's only desire was to conclude peace as gracefully as possible, whatever the outcome at New Orleans.

The raid on the French port of Dieppe in July, 1942, has always been treated as a major disaster with virtually no redeeming aspects, but Lieutenant Colonel Daniel Webb has sought to find some value in the experience in his article on "The Dieppe Raid—An Act of Diplomacy" (*Military Review,* LX, 1980, 31-37). Webb argues that the Allies secured vital information that helped in the planning of amphibious assaults to come, and that the raid represented a pledge to the Russians that we would work to divert German forces from the Russian front. What Webb overlooks is that a brief, unsuccessful raid could only add to the Germans' confidence that their harbor defenses were sufficient. A diversion of troops from the Eastern front could be achieved only by a landing and a sustained occupation of territory, forcing the Germans to gather troops to expel the invaders. The Allies made no such effort until the Normandy landings of 1944, a fact the Soviets still remember.

Another military operation that turns out to have had no intended political purpose is the subject of Harriette Chandler's "Another View of Operation Crossword: A Revision of Kolko (*Military Affairs,* XLII, 1978, 68–74). The attempts to achieve an early German surrender in Northern Italy in 1945 were part of a conspiracy by the Anglo-Americans to prevent local Communists from dominating northern Italy. Chandler utilizes documents declassified since Kolko's work appeared to show that in fact the primary motivation remained military. There simply was no reason to continue to lose lives in the northern Italian theater in March, 1945, and a German surrender there could open the door for the unconditional surrender of the remaining German armies. The Allies feared that a Soviet presence in the negotiations would cause the Germans to continue fighting; thus the exclusion of the Soviets should not be viewed as a Cold War conspiracy.

In his study of Civil War policy making, "1861: Blockade vs. Closing the Confederate Ports" (*Military Affairs,* XLI, 1977, 190–194) Stuart Anderson demonstrates that the choice of military operations may have had diplomatic consequences. Secretary of the Navy Gideon Welles tried to persuade President Abraham Lincoln that a blockade of the Confederacy would necessarily involve granting belligerent rights to the Rebels. That would contradict the administration's claim that secession was an impossibility and that therefore no actual war, in the legal sense, could take place. Welles recommended that the President issue an edict closing the Southern ports to all ships. Anderson's research in the British sources demonstrates that blockade was the correct choice. The British were willing to accept a blockade applied within the rules of international law, but they would have regarded the closure of ports as an illegal "paper blockade" which they would have had to defy. Thus Welles' choice of military policy could have led straight to European intervention and the destruction of the Union.

It is certainly reasonable to expect historians to follow the trail of recently opened documents. But there is another area of the history of national security policy which is being sadly neglected. The first attempts to coordinate diplomatic, naval, and military policy occurred in the years following the Spanish-American War. Machinery for coordination, such as the Army-Navy Joint Board, appeared at that time. It is a period and a topic that deserve far more study than they are receiving, since the foundations of our current national security machinery were laid in these years.

Scholars have not completely ignored the period. Dean Allard examines "Anglo-American Naval Difference During World War I" (*Military Affairs*, XLIV, 1980, 75–81). He finds that even when the United States was part of a military alliance, it still insisted on an independent policy, one which was reflected in its naval operations. Kendrick Clements finds cause to praise "Woodrow Wilson's Mexican Policy, 1913–1915" (*Diplomatic History*, IV, 1980, 113–136), concluding that it was far more successful and intelligent than historians have admitted. Wilson steered a delicate course that helped Mexico realize true independence without foreign domination. Certainly that is a controversial conclusion, but perhaps it will help to rekindle interest in the period. The period deserves attention because it marks the time when American leaders first became aware of the need to coordinate military and foreign policies because of our participation in world politics on a regular basis. Historians have always been comfortable when dealing with wartime diplomacy, or the impact of wars on the home front. Perhaps the time has come to acknowledge that the study of military institutions in peacetime is as essential to an understanding of our past as is the study of these institutions in wartime.

Future Directions in Research

Vietnam will undoubtedly continue to fascinate American historians, because it appears more and more to be a watershed in the history of U.S. strategic policies. The study of the war should receive a boost as the various branches begin to publish their official service histories of the war. The authors of these studies have access to classified documents in many cases, thus their works can at least hint at further information to come. That was one of the most valuable aspects of the official army histories of the Second World War. Interest in the Korean War is increasing because of current publication of official histories and the declassification of records.

Already benefiting from the recent declassification of military records is the study of U.S. weapons development. This is the topic of two recent articles. Gregg Herken's " 'A Most Deadly Illusion': The Atomic Secret and American Nuclear Weapons Policy, 1945–1950" (*Pacific Historical Review*, XLIX, 1980, 51–76) examines the trauma suffered by American policy makers when the Soviet Union exploded an atomic bomb. One immediate effect of the Soviet bomb was the Truman administration's decision to proceed with development of the hydrogen bomb. But Herken

argues there were political and psychological effects of even greater importance. U.S. policy makers had expected to enjoy a nuclear monopoly for as
long as 20 years after the war, a monopoly that would provide complete
security in world affairs. The surprising Russian success destroyed the
basis for existing U.S. military policy, and its psychological impact caused
Americans to ignore their own intelligence failure and seek scapegoats in
the scientific community, setting the stage for the McCarthy era. In addition, by dwelling on the possibility of espionage, American policy makers
could avoid dealing with the fundamental problems in their approach to
world affairs. The development of the hydrogen bomb was supposed to
recreate the security that had been lost. This search for total security
through nuclear weapons led instead to an accelerated arms race and diminished security.

David Alan Rosenberg examines the military's role in the "American
Atomic Strategy and the Hydrogen Bomb Decision (*Journal of American
History*, LXVI, 1979, 62-87). Rosenberg finds that the Joint Chiefs of
Staff based their planning on a vastly exaggerated sense of Russian conventional capability. When the Soviets added an atomic bomb to their existing
conventional forces, the Joint Chiefs began to fear that the U.S. military
was too weak to support American foreign policy objectives. Thus the
military leadership was eager to proceed with research and development of
the hydrogen bomb, even though they lacked a clear idea of how to use the
weapon when it became available. Rosenberg concludes that while the
development of the hydrogen bomb and the conventional rearmament of
the Korean War period may have been political responses to specific
events, nevertheless these policy choices were based on an abiding set of
attitudes about national security.

American military history has concentrated its research on the Civil
War, World War II, and the Revolution, and has therefore left much room
for further research and study in previously neglected periods. As any
reader of today's newspapers can attest, military force continues to be an
important part of human relations; if historians are to understand the past
better, they must continue to study the military, war, and diplomacy.

Thomas R. English is on the faculty of the Foxcroft School.

Journals Consulted

*Aerospace Historian • American Historical Review • American Jewish
Historical Quarterly • The American Scholar • American Quarterly •*

Armed Forces and Society • Asia Quarterly • Australian Journal of Politics and History • Daedalus • Diplomatic History • Foreign Affairs • The Historian • Journal of American History • Journal of Interamerican Studies and World Affairs • Journal of Modern History • Journal of Negro History • Journal of Peace Research • Journal of the History of Ideas • Labor History • Military Affairs • Military Review • Pacific Historical Review • Phylon • Political Science Quarterly • Prologue • Utah Historical Quarterly • William and Mary Quarterly • Wilson Quarterly • Wisconsin Magazine of History • World Politics • Yale Review.

THE UNITED STATES:
THE SOCIAL HISTORY OF THE
MILITARY TO 1940

Edward M. Coffman

In 1912, the American Historical Association included a session on military history in its annual convention program. At this meeting the civilian and military panelists surveyed the field and bemoaned the lack of interest and the insufficiency of competent scholarly works. R. M. Johnston of Harvard said that the mini-course he offered intermittently was the only military history course he believed to be available in American universities. He and others also noted that the military itself paid little attention to its history.

The question of definition did not come up. Apparently all present understood that military history was concerned with the conduct of war. The only speaker who called for broadening that approach was one who automatically received special consideration, not only because he was president of the AHA, but more so because he was Theodore Roosevelt. The former President also assumed that military history was a study of wartime maneuvers but he added: "I don't believe it is possible to treat military history as something entirely apart from the general national history" (*Annual Report of the American Historical Association,* 1912, 190). In particular, he emphasized the need for investigating national attitudes toward the military.

Since 1912, the United States has fought two World Wars, emerged as a military superpower and, for the last 35 years, has been caught up in the waxing and waning of a Cold War which turned hot in Korea and Vietnam. During these years military history has increased in popularity. Although the hostility of a liberal society toward the study of war, which Professor Johnston noted, still exists in academe (one finds little evidence of the military in the *Journal of Social History* for example), the number of military history books one sees on drugstore bookstands is a testament to the popular appeal of the subject. So too is the flourishing of organizations for enthusiasts. While membership of Civil War Round Tables may have declined since the centennial years, such groups as World War I Aero Historians and the Council of Abandoned Military Posts (members of which are interested not only in the sites of military installations but in the lives of the occupants) rally enthusiasts of similar interest and publish their research in *Cross and Cockade, Heliogram,* and the CAMP *Periodical.* Some scholars might dismiss such articles as antiquarian but they are valuable for the specialized knowledge they reflect and, on occasion, as is the case with commemorative unit histories, as primary sources. Even in institutions of higher learning, as Professor Johnston might be surprised to find, military history courses have burgeoned (John A. Lynn, "Military History in the Classroom: A Strategy for Enrollment" [*Military Affairs,* XLIII, 1979, 202–204]). Certainly he would be pleased to know that the military history society and the scholarly journal which he called for have existed, in the form of the American Military Institute and *Military Affairs,* for more than 40 years.

Much of the current interest is, understandably, in World War II and the Vietnam War. Aside from being the major military benchmarks in the lives of most Americans, these two wars occasioned extensive sociological and psychological studies. During the past two decades, the field of military sociology, in particular, has blossomed under the leadership of Morris Janowitz. Janowitz brought together like-minded historians, political scientists, and sociologists in the Interuniversity Seminar on Armed Forces and Society, which publishes the quarterly *Armed Forces and Society.* In addition to this publication, there is also the *Journal of Political and Military Sociology,* concerned essentially with post-1940 matters. For historians, the work of these social scientists provides a wealth of material about the American military since 1940. With some exceptions, notably the extensive intelligence testing program of World War I and various medical studies, such efforts are lacking for the pre-1940 era.

There is another characteristic which separates the American military since 1940 from the past. Since the mobilization for World War II, the military has never returned to the periphery of American political, economic, and social life in the peacetime intervals as it did in the past. The proportion of military men in the total labor force peaked in peacetime during the 19th century at .05 per cent in 1820 and in the first four decades of the 20th century at .08 per cent in 1920, while the nadir during the Cold War was 2.3 per cent in 1950 (Peter Karsten, *Soldiers and Society: The Effects of Military Service and War on American Life,* Westport, Conn., 1978, 11)—an indication of the difference in importance that only hints at the much larger degree of public attention the military has received since World War II. The Cold War has blurred the distinctions between war and peace as well as between civil and military, areas which seemed so clear before. One could also argue that the great technological advances of the last 40 years have made history prior to that irrelevant to policy makers. Meanwhile commentators find the examples of warfare and the good war-bad war contrast, which the World War II and Vietnam experiences afford, sufficient for their needs.

Despite the richness of data and the popularity of the World War II and postwar period, there remains a good deal of interest not only in American military history generally, prior to 1940, but also in the social aspects of that history. In May 1979, the National Archives made a strong affirmation of that in its conference "Soldiers and Civilians: The United States Army and the American People," where a large majority of the papers dealt with social ramifications of the army prior to World War II (Garry D. Ryan and Timothy K. Nenninger are currently preparing the volume of proceedings for publication). Over the last dozen years, the biennial military history symposia at the U.S. Air Force Academy have also had a fair representation of papers which fall into that broad area, while almost all of the papers in the 1976 symposium "The American Military on the Frontier" (which appeared in book form edited by James P. Tate in 1978) were in that category.

More recent significant manifestations of this interest were published in the spring of 1980. Arno Press has brought out an impressive series, *The American Military Experience*, consisting of 43 books. The editor, Richard H. Kohn, included among the reprints a sizeable number of perceptively chosen pre-World War II memoirs and documents of social interest. Of five previously unpublished doctoral dissertations, three—including Richard C. Brown's influential *Social Attitudes of American Generals, 1898-1940*— are from that period. Also from the pre-World War II period are the anthology *Anglo-American Antimilitary Tracts, 1697-1830* and a large part of the selection of military laws (*Military Laws of the United States, from the Civil War through the War Powers Act of 1973*) which Kohn edited for this series. While this large collection should prove a boon to libraries as well as individuals interested in these hard-to-find volumes, the other publication was meant for the classroom market. Peter Karsten, whose *Naval Aristocracy* (1972) and collection of documents (*Soldiers and Society: The Effects of Military Service and War on American Life, 1978*) have earned him a place among the leaders in the field, has brought out *The Military in America From the Colonial Era to the Present*. This paperback is a collection of monographs and documents about such matters as

> the social origins of military personnel, the process of socialization and value inculcation in the military environment, public attitudes toward military systems, military attitudes toward the public, the relation of military to economic and political elites, the development of interservice rivalries, or the effect of military service on the individual.

Of the 42 selections, more than two-thirds are concerned with the pre-1940 era. While recent research predominates, two of the scholarly pieces first appeared in the 1920s. Not surprisingly, since the Civil War has evoked so much interest through the years, these selections by E. Merton Coulter and Ella Lonn attempt respectively to explain why Kentuckians chose to support or oppose the Union and the causes of Confederate desertions. The editor also pays tribute in his preface to two social-history classics about the Civil War which are old in scholarly terms but certainly not outdated—Bell Irvin Wiley's *The Life of Johnny Reb* (1943) and *The Life of Billy Yank* (1951). He also praises Dixon Wecter's *When Johnny Comes Marching Home* (1944), still the best study of demobilization after the American wars.

Scholars have done excellent work in social history for many years, as Wiley and Wecter illustrate in the particular area of the military, yet recently the field appears to be more in vogue among academics. In part this may be a result of its amorphous characteristics. The whimsical definition of social history as history with politics left out, which can be adapted to military history by substituting battles for politics, might not be generally accepted, but then one searches in vain for a consensual definition. As James A. Henretta, Darrett B. Rutman, and Robert F. Berkhofer, Jr. reveal in "Social History As Lived And Written: AHR Forum" (*American Historical Review*, LXXXIV, 1979, 1293–1333), the field is characterized by diverse aims and methods. For some, the computer offers the hope of learning more about the lot of the presumably inarticulate common man by making use of the myriad statistics collected by government agencies. With the computer, however, there is the tendency for practitioners to become caught up in the convolutions of mathematical and social-scientific theories and to produce articles which impress non-devotees as being more concerned with theory and method than with history. Besides, there is an obvious distortion of the warp and woof of life if description is limited to what has been or can be counted.

The quantitative approach, nevertheless, remains an invaluable tool which social historians can use to supplement traditional research. One reason for the ascendancy of quantitative history among academic social historians is the belief that letters, diaries, records, memoirs—so-called literary material—simply do not exist in sufficient quantity or quality about most people to enable scholars to ask the questions which they could ask of elites. The numerous letters and diaries which Wiley used in his books on Civil War soldiers might be dismissed as a phenomenon peculiar to that war, but scholars who are better acquainted with military sources know that there is a wealth of material available about the common man in uniform. The answer to almost any question a social historian could devise about soldiers' lives is in the military files because the military bureaucracy created and maintained records about its people to an extent that one rarely finds in civilian society.

Before the era of censorship and the prohibition of diary-keeping (another World War II distinction), the Civil War and its successors were more productive of personal records. Events inspired a sense of history, and the thousands upon thousands of civilians temporarily turned soldier or sailor wanted to keep in touch with their families and friends. This is in contrast to the peacetime regulars. The latter composed only a fraction of the number of those serving in war, and they were also less likely to have people they wanted to correspond with. Such men were more interested in getting away from, rather than with maintaining, contact with family and friends.

Diligent searching, however, will turn up more personal material on the pre-1900 peacetime regular than one might presume available, while personal contact with post-1900 veterans through correspondence and interviews can answer many social history questions. Don Rickey Jr. in *Forty Miles: A Day on Beans and Hay* (Norman, Oklahoma, 1963) pushed the time barrier back a quarter of a century by contacting Indian War veterans in the 1950s. Later, he made another significant contribution to military social history by organizing a survey of Spanish-American War veterans. This survey brought into a research library, the U.S. Army Military History Institute at Carlisle Barracks, Pennsylvania, the letters, diaries and, through interviews, memories of survivors of that war.

In addition to whatever personal sources can be located, the official records contain millions of pages of data. In regard to the army, for example, post records delineate the routine and show what was available in the library and on the shelves of the sutler's store; court-martial and medical records add considerably to an understanding of what life was like in an isolated fort beyond the edge of what was considered civilization. Reports of various kinds and the correspondence which frequently takes the form of complaints or appeals add depth to the portrait of the small society of a hundred or so in a frontier fort. There are also personnel records which in the 19th century fall beyond the realm of classification. Enlistment registers provide a few descriptive details and space for only a few words about service. Beginning in the 1860s, the appointment, commission, and promotion files of officers contain a wealth of information in the variety of records or correspondence which the officer or the army deemed relevant to his career. Although some scholars have probed the treasure trove of official records, they are so extensive that large segments remain virtually untouched. A general description should indicate the possibilities inherent in this material.

More convenient than these manuscript records (some of which are available, however, in microfilm publications) are the annual published reports and officers' registers which after the Civil War began to contain some biographical data. For those who study officers' careers, limited data—place of birth and appointment, dates of ranks, units assigned to, and dates of discharge, resignation, retirement, and death for officers who served prior to 1903—are available in Frances B. Heitman, *Historical Register and Dictionary of the United States Army, from its Organization, September 29, 1789 to March 2, 1903* (1903; reprinted 1965). There is more detail available on the careers of West Pointers in their alumni registers initiated by George W. Cullum in 1868 and added to in periodic supplements (*Biographical Register of Officers and Graduates of the United States Military Academy at West Point, N.Y.,* 3 volumes, 1868).

The publication of newly discovered primary sources is prevalent in the field. Certainly historians have reason to appreciate having sources made readily available and, presumably, they will make use of them in the preparation of future monographs. The most noteworthy of these discoveries is the work of John C. Dann. He had the imagination to look for memoirs among the pension applications of Revolutionary War veterans and the perseverance to go through those thousands of pages. He found what he was looking for, as a few of those veterans elaborated on their service records to include details of experiences and observations. Among them were boys, blacks, and one woman. Sarah Osborn, who accompanied her husband to the war thus becomes the only known woman who left a reminiscence of her experiences with the Continental Army. Excerpts from this collection appeared under the title "The Revolution Remembered" in a recent *American Heritage* (XXXI, 1980, 49–64), while the book with the same title came out in the spring of 1980. Another document of the Revolutionary War which poses some interesting questions is a militia return of a New Jersey company that includes the names of 19 women along with the 95 men. Is this evidence of female conscription? Military units of that day customarily carried women along as laundresses, but there are too many for that purpose and several are not wives. Just what were they doing on such a roster? Harriet Stryker-Rodda, who published the document in *Daughters of the American Revolution Magazine* (CXIII, 1979, 308–312) did not know.

Among the other publications, three pertain to medical aspects of the military, an area which military social historians have long found fruitful. Pharmacy historians, such as Rudolf Schmitz, summarize their findings of the medical records of Hessian units during the Revolutionary War in "The Medical and Pharmaceutical Care of Hessian Troops During the American War of Independence", in *American Pharmacy in the Colonial and Revolutionary Periods* (ed. George A. Benda and John Parascandola, 1977, 37–47). The prescription books and other medical records of Fort Laramie are described by Anthony Palmieri III and Daniel J. Hammond in "Drug Therapy at a Frontier Fort Hospital: Fort Laramie, Wyoming Territory, 1870–1889" (*Pharmacy in History*, XXI, 1979, 35–44). The third article is a summary of the wartime diary of a Civil War Army doctor supplemented by some biographical information (Philip D. Jordan, "The Career of Henry M. Farr, Civil War Surgeon" [*Annals of Iowa,* XLIV, 1978, 191–211]). In the same issue Glenda Riley has published "Civil War Wife: The Letters of Harriet Jane Thompson" (214–231, 296–314). These letters from a wife to her husband, a major in an Iowa regiment, reflect the current interest not only in women's history but also in the impact of war on non-combatants.

The publication of such documents is a characteristic of local history journals and indicates a basic appeal of social history—be it related to the fort in the vicinity, to a veteran's experiences, or to strictly civilian concerns—which has not waned. At the grassroots there is little, if any, interest in the complex debates which occupy some academic historians but great enthusiasm for the inherent fascination of the material. Two articles in *Military History of Texas and the Southwest* reflect this interest in military social history. In an article entitled "The Commissary Sergeant: His Life at Fort Davis" (XIV, 1978, 21–32), Doug McChristian defines commissary sergeants, explains their jobs at frontier posts, and provides some details about the men who held that position at Fort Davis from 1873 to 1891. Since one would have to look long and hard to find anything else in historical literature about this important non-commissioned officer, this brief article does fill a gap. Joan Ingalles was enthralled by "Family Life on the Southwest Frontier" (XIV, 1978, 203-213) and has written a description of it primarily from published memoirs. This aspect of the military frontier is portrayed, however, in much more depth by Patricia Y. Stallard in *Glittering Misery: Dependents of the Indian Fighting Army* (Novato, Calif., 1978), who does for the women and children of the post-Civil War frontier army what Rickey (*Forty Miles*) had done for the soldiers. She was unable to make personal contacts, as Rickey did, but she skillfully uses manuscripts and unpublished records to supplement the published memoirs and other sources to depict the life of these people. An unusual document is a fragment covering less than four months of a 1790s post record. Such items are rare even in the National Archives because of a fire in 1800 which destroyed many of the army records. "An Orderly Book from Fort Washington and Fort Hamilton, 1792-1793" which David A. Simmons has published in *The Cincinnati Historical Society Bulletin* (XXXVI, 1978, 125-144) contains entries about clothing and fuel issues, pay, training, punishments, and the celebration of Christmas (which meant an extra gill of whiskey ration to each soldier).

Another monograph on the peacetime Army might well be considered by Pentagon policy makers who deal with the problems of a volunteer army. In "Quality Not Quantity: The Volunteer Army During the Depression" (*Military Affairs*, XLIII, 1979, 171-177) Robert K. Griffith, Jr. describes and analyzes army recruiting during the 1930s. Based on thorough research in War Department records, Griffith's article shows that although the declining economy induced more volunteers initially, the New Deal relief measures changed this situation. Military social historians can look forward to Griffith's forthcoming book, *Men Wanted for the U.S. Army: The Volunteer Army and American Society, 1919-1940,* as a solid contribution to the field.

William B. Skelton, who gave one of the papers at the National Archives Conference, is currently at work on what promises to be the definitive study of army officers from the 1780s to the Civil War. His most recent effort, "Officers and Politicians: The Origins of Army Politics in the United States before the Civil War" (*Armed Forces and Society,* VI, 1979, 22-48), reflects exhaustive research. Skelton explains that the officer corps, which was ostensibly aloof from politics was, in reality, very active in the political sphere. The officers' activity, however, was principally in the interest of professional goals. They sought to further their individual careers, their particular branches, or the army itself. Using a successful blend of historical and sociological methods, he demonstrates that the controversial patterns of military politics in recent years actually emerged prior to the Civil War.

Wars, as one would expect, dominate the study of military social history; after all, they are the times of greatest national involvement in military matters. Research in the Revolutionary War period has produced at least two recent articles which come under the social rubric. In an article on "Robert Morris and the Courts-Martial of Captains Samuel Nicholson and John Manley of the Continental Navy" (*Military Affairs*, XLIV, 1980, 13-17) Stephen T. Powers uses two courts-martial of naval officers as a commentary on navy morale. Paul D. Nelson analyzes the attitudes of Revolutionary War generals toward regulars and militia in his "Citizen Soldiers or Regulars: The Views of American General Officers on the Military Establishment, 1775-1781" (*Military Affairs,* XLIII, 1979, 126-132) which sets the scene for a debate that ranged throughout American history. Two scholars who deal with World War I topics are interested in the effect of the war on society. David J. Pivar's "Cleansing the Nation: The War on Prostitution, 1917-21" (*Prologue*, XII, 1980, 29-40) examines the social engineering attempt to deal with venereal disease and prostitution—an effort which shows how the Progressive spirit and method carried over into the war. In "Southern Women in the War: The North Carolina Woman's Committee, 1917-1919" (*North Carolina Historical Review*, LV, 1978, 251-283) William J. Breen goes beyond a description of the activities of this organization to suggest the war's effect on the position of women in Southern society and on social reform in that region.

The participation of minorities in the military is another area of interest in social history. Frederick S. Harrod, in an article on "Jim Crow in the Navy, 1798-1941" (*U.S. Naval Institute Proceedings*, CV, 1979, 46-53), traces the place of blacks in that service and details how the navy followed the lead of civilian society by increasing restrictions on blacks during the first four decades of this century. Harrod has adapted this piece from his model study, *Manning the New Navy: The Development of a Modern Naval Enlisted Force, 1899-1940* (Westport, Conn., 1978).

There were also Indians in the American Army. In "Indian Soldiers of the 36th Division" (*Military History of Texas and the Southwest*, XV, 1979, 7-20) Lonnie White uses published sources to describe the composition and actions of the 600 or so Indians in the Oklahoma and Texas National Guard Division during World War I. At the time, these Indians, who were mostly Choctaws, received much publicity because of their race and wealth. One company with a sizeable number of oil and land rich Indians was called the Millionaire Company; they served in integrated units and excelled in sports as well as in combat. Thomas Dunlap deals with Indians in the more customary format of the frontier wars but his focus is neither on the Indians nor the wars. Rather it is on the attitudes of General George Crook, who condemned the disregard of Indian rights and the whites' maltreatment of the Indians. Although Crook's views are well known among specialists, Dunlap thoughtfully puts them in context in "General Crook and the White Man Problem" (*Journal of the West*, XVII, 1979, 3-10).

By broadening the scope of military social history to include the interaction of the military and war with society, possibilities of research become virtually limitless. Two of the previously cited articles are in this category and there are others worth noting which have appeared recently. In "Privateers and Prize Cases: The Impact Upon Nova Scotia, 1775-83" (*Prologue*, XI, 1979, 185-199) John D. Faibisy relies primarily on legal records to illustrate the effect that privateering had on Nova Scotia during the Revolutionary War. Faibisy concludes that American raids on Nova Scotian shipping and the unfair treatment of Nova Scotian claims in American maritime courts killed any hope of colonial cooperation with the emerging revolutionary movement in Nova Scotia. Two other authors describe the relationship of universities—MIT and Oklahoma State—with the military over the years: Philip R. Rulon, "The Campus Cadets: A History of Collegiate Military Training 1891-1951" (*Chronicles of Oklahoma*, LVII, 1979, 67-90) and Jack H. Nunn, "MIT: A University's Contributions to National Defense" (*Military Affairs*, XLIII, 1979, 120-125). Both authors summarize the history of military training and discuss the effect of the two world wars and the development of defense research programs on their institutions. Rulon also discusses OSU's experience with World War II veterans.

The relationship between civilian communities and military bases as well as the effects of war on a particular town offer some of the most interesting topics in the recent literature. Donna Thomas explains the influence of Miami boosters on the Army's decision to build a temporary camp there in 1898 and then discusses the not too pleasant results of that effort ("'Camp Hell': Miami During the Spanish-American War" [*Florida Historical Quarterly*, LVII, 1978, 141-156]). A new town of some 2,000 in 1898, Miami had difficulty in coping with a large camp. Its lack of facilities, contributing to civil-military friction, low morale, and sickness among the soldiers, reflected the shortsightedness of the boosters. Donald

W. White has done a more extensive study of how a New Jersey town weathered the Revolutionary War. His article on "A Local History Approach to the American Revolution: Chatham, New Jersey" (*New Jersey History*, XCVI, 1978, 49-64) gives an indication of the scope of his book, *A Village At War: Chatham, New Jersey and the American Revolution* (Madison, N.J., 1979). Away from the corridors of power and the battlefields, these ordinary people, who are never ordinary when one looks at them closely, wanted to be let alone and showed a reluctance to change. This study of their experiences, reactions, and attitudes goes far toward humanizing this turbulent period, and that is a virtue of well done grassroots history.

In two recent articles which overlap somewhat, "The City and the Sword: San Francisco and The Rise of the Metropolitan-Military Complex, 1919-1941" (*Journal of American History*, LXV, 1979, 996-1020) and "The Metropolitan-Military Complex in Comparative Perspective: San Francisco, Los Angeles, and San Diego, 1919-1941" (*Journal of the West*, XVIII, 1979, 19-30), Roger W. Lotchin deals with the fascinating relationship of military and ubran developments in California during the two decades between the world wars. Although the military-industrial complex has received a good deal of publicity and resulted in some scholarship, this topic has not attracted the attention it deserves. On the West Coast, after World War I, military (mostly naval officers) and civic leaders found that their goals could be attained through cooperation. The military's desire for bases had obvious economic benefits for neighboring cities. Lotchin examines what he terms the "military welfarism" which results from the pump-priming economic effect of placing military bases near cities. Local leaders in these California cities thought that the Federal money brought in by these bases would fill the economic gap caused by the lack of industry. His articles correct the view that the West Coast military-industrial alliance began in World War II.

This sampling of recent literature indicates that scholars no longer have the narrow view of military history that their predecessors accepted in 1912. Armies and navies do not cease to exist between wars and, during those conflicts, they have effects that are not limited to the battlefield. Historians now understand that and are seizing the opportunities for research made possible by this broader view. New research fields to conquer might well include the possibilities of collective biography which military personnel records offer, for military social historians have made use of the quantitative tools which would be particularly of value in such analysis. Others might investigate urban-military connections such as Lotchin did in

California in the 1920s and 1930s. It is difficult to describe and analyze the complex social, political, and economic connections but, if well done, such work would go far toward destroying stereotypes which have hampered public understanding of the military.

Finally, students of the military, along with most of their colleagues in other areas of history, have been remiss in not putting their particular subject into context and in not making comparisons. The saying that the military mirrors society is well known and frequently ignored. Marcus Cunliffe used this comparative approach to great advantage when he dismantled the shibboleth of the Southern military tradition in his landmark study, *Soldiers and Civilians: The Martial Spirit In America, 1775–1865* (New York, 1968). Theodore Roosevelt pointed the way when he told that 1912 gathering that they should not isolate military history from general national history. Those acquainted with the military history field now know that it no longer wears a uniform and that it is indeed flourishing in the social area.

Edward M. Coffman is on the faculty of the University of Wisconsin.

Journals Consulted

American Heritage • American Historical Review • Annals of Iowa • Armed Forces and Society • Chronicles of Oklahoma • Cincinnati Historical Society Bulletin • Daughters of the American Revolution Magazine • Florida Historical Quarterly • Journal of American History • Journal of Political and Military Sociology • Journal of Social History • Journal of the West • Military Affairs • Military History of Texas and the Southwest • Military Images • New Jersey History • North Carolina Historical Review • Pharmacy in History • Prologue • U.S. Naval Institute Proceedings.

INDEX OF PERSONAL NAMES

INDEX OF SUBJECTS